In The Morning, I'd like to encourage you to journal your own thoughts after each devotional. It's my prayer that your entire year will be filled with blessings, peace, love, and joy. May you always know that **In The Morning,** You shall rise again.

Sincerely,
Travasa

IN THE MORNING

TRAVASA HOLLOWAY

TNHB Inspirations
Rock Hill, South Carolina

IN THE MORNING

Published by
TNHB Inspirations
Rock Hill, SC.
tnhb@tnhb-inspirations.com

Editorial Services TNHB Inspirations LLC

Cover Design courtesy of Fredrick Fluker enfocus Media Group
Yvonne Rose/Qualitypress.info – Book Packager

All Rights Reserved

No part of this book may be reproduced or transmitted in any form or by any means, unless permission is obtained by the author.

The content provided herein is for informational and inspirational purposes only and does not take place of any medical consultations.

Copyright © 2021 Travasa Holloway
ISBN# 978-0-578-99243-3
Library of Congress Control Number: 2021917978

DEDICATION

I dedicate this writing journey to Barbara Holloway.

My beloved Grandmother, but the woman who raised me that I call Mamma.

Thank you for EVERYTHING.

ACKNOWLEDGEMENTS

With gratitude, I thank God for not taking His hands off me when I wanted to let go. I realize the gift that I have to encourage others, and I'm grateful for the angels that He has encompassed around me when I need an encouraging Word to get through my day. With Love, I thank you, and I love you to life.

Ra'Mon & Rod Holloway

>Willie L. Stevens
>
>The Holloway Ladies
>*(Barbara, Brenda, Carla, Khara & Tekeye)*
>
>Pastor Rabon L. & Mia Turner
>*(Grace Emmanuel Baptist Church of Flint MI)*
>
>Pastor Tyshawn & Shonetay Gardner
>*(Plum Grove Baptist Church of Tuscaloosa AL)*
>
>Dr. Derrol & Patricia H. Dawkins
>*(New Start Covenant of Grace of Birmingham AL)*
>
>Pastor Leroy & Tina Caudle
>*(Eagles Nest Cathedral International of Huntsville AL)*
>
>Bishop Daniel J. & Tiffany Richardson
>*(Eagles Nest Cathedral International of Huntsville AL)*
>
>Family & Friends

CONTENTS

Dedication..i
Acknowledgements...iii
Contents...v
Preface xvii
In The Morning..xvii
Introduction xix

Devotionals: 365 Days of TNHB Inspirations............................1
January 1st: "Unstoppable"..2
January 2nd: "For The Right Reasons" 3
January 3rd: "But The Year Changed".......................................4
January 4th: "Don't Forfeit What Has Been Purposed" 5
January 5th: "Stop Trying To Steal The Pen"...........................6
January 6th: "Stop Asking Blind People To Proofread Your Vision"...........7
January 7th: "But It's Not Attractive"......................................8
January 8th: "The Apology You'll Never Get" 9
January 9th: "Digging Up Doubt" 10
January 10th: "Step Out Of The Race" 11
January 11th: "Like Husks Falling Off Corn" 12
January 12th: "It's Your Path" 13
January 13th: Talk is Cheap! "But The Consequences Are Expensive" 14
January 14th: "Send Them A Thank You Card" 15
January 15th: "A Bad Landing" 16
January 16th: "Waiting For The Snails To Come Into The Ark" 17
January 17th: "Noise Maker" 18
January 18th: "Snooze You Lose" 19
January 19th: "It's What You Need"......................................20
January 20th: "What Hurt You, Doesn't Have To Haunt You" 21
January 21st: "The Villain" 22
January 22nd: "Trained To Complain"....................................23
January 23rd: "Pleading My Case"..24

January 24th: "It's Okay To Be The Tortoise" 25
January 25th: "Appreciation Day" 26
January 26th: "Stop The Advice & Audience" 27
January 27th: "Put Your Fence Up" 28
January 28th: "I Need A New Pencil" 29
January 29th: "Prayer Warrior vs. Prayer Worrier" 30
January 30th: "The Alligator On The Ladder" 31
January 31st: "Digging Back Up Your Seed" 32

February 1st: "Keeping The Infection From Spreading" 33
February 2nd: "Cancel Your Subscription" 34
February 3rd: "But I'm Part-Time" 35
February 4th: "Grow In The Dirt" 36
February 5th: "The Red Muscle in Your Mouth" 37
February 6th: "The Conditions Have Changed" 38
February 7th: "You Didn't Fail, You Fell" 39
February 8th: "Raggedy to Royalty" 40
February 9th: "Keep Reading" 41
February 10th: "But You Stepped On Them Though" 42
February 11th: "At The Breaking Point" 43
February 12th: "Put Them On Your Prayer List" 44
February 13th: "Just Don't" 45
February 14th: "I'm Too Disappointed" 46
February 15th: "Everything Is Working Against Me" 47
February 16th: "I Have A Problem" 48
February 17th: "You're Attacking Me" 49
February 18th: "Remember, God Forgives YOU" 50
February 19th: "If Only The Mouth Was Closed" 51
February 20th: "It's Okay To Say No" 52
February 21st: "Eyes Fixed on God" 53
February 22nd: "Pain, Not The Preferred Teacher" 54
February 23rd: "5+4=9" 55
February 24th: "The Gift Isn't For Everybody" 56
February 25th: "You Owe Yourself An Apology" 57

February 26th: "No Thank You" 58
February 27th: "You're Not Finished" 59
February 28th: "The Lions You Face" 60

March 1st: "Hurt Happens" 61
March 2nd: "Planting Weeds Won't Bloom Flowers 62
March 3rd: "Know When To Get Up" 63
March 4th: "Pretty Words" 64
March 5th: "Be Teachable" 65
March 6th: "A Recipe For Unhappiness" 66
March 7th: "You're Not Being Punished" 67
March 8th: "Why Won't You Do Something" 68
March 9th: "A Necessary Wreck" 69
March 10th: "Disguised As What You Want" 70
March 11th: "A Lie is Nothing Without Power" 71
March 12th: "Not Everyone's Choice" 72
March 13th: "You Can't Change Them" 73
March 14th: "Suffering in Silence" 74
March 15th: "Chaos Addiction or Peace" 75
March 16th: "A Divine Appointment" 76
March 17th: "God Has Something Better For Me" 77
March 18th: "A Repeated Cycle" 78
March 19th: "I'm Not Ready For This" 79
March 20th: "The Revenge Isn't Worth It" 80
March 21st: "But Is It Healthy?" 81
March 22nd: "It's Overdue" 82
March 23rd: "(THIS) That I'm Going Through" 83
March 24th: "The Banana Peels on The Ground" 84
March 25th: "God Told Me To Tell You..." 85
March 26th: "But I Told You My Pain" 86
March 27th: "The Fight Of My Life" 87
March 28th: "Burying The Pain" 88
March 29th: "The Message" 89
March 30th: "Where's The Focus" 90

March 31st: "Band-Aids Won't Fix It" 91
April 1st: "It's Your Response That Counts" 92
April 2nd: "Protect Your Peace, PERIOD" 93
April 3rd: "Take a Look in The Mirror" 94
April 4th: "Prison of Paradise" 95
April 5th: "Weapons or Medicine" 96
April 6th: "We're On Different Pages" 97
April 7th: "They Will Never Give It To You" 98
April 8th: "Mean What You Say & Say What You Mean" 99
April 9th: "It's Just Childish" 100
April 10th: "A Victim of Absence" 101
April 11th: "Did You Let It Go or Bury It?" 102
April 12th: "Let It Rain" 103
April 13th: "What Is Your Attitude Saying?" 104
April 14th: "Use Your Keys Wisely" 105
April 15th: "Walking Around With Scissors" 106
April 16th: "They've Moved On" 107
April 17th: "Your "YES" Doesn't Need Counsel" 108
April 18th: "The Letdown" 109
April 19th: "Committed To The Deadline or Delay?" 110
April 20th: "Sabotaging The Ship" 111
April 21st: "A Protected Heart" 112
April 22nd: "The Stalker" 113
April 23rd: "But You Got What You Wanted" 114
April 24th: "Are You Going To Be In Faith or In Your Feelings?" 115
April 25th: "Their Opinion But Your Assignment" 116
April 26th: "Out of VIP" 117
April 27th: "The Obsession" 118
April 28th: "Let Them Be Mad" 119
April 29th: "Fight For It" 120
April 30th: "The Ear That Listens" 121

May 1st: "The Know-It-All" 122
May 2nd: "Just Say NO!" 123

May 3rd: "The Anointed" 124
May 4th: "Take The Medicine Please" 125
May 5th: "I Need To Lose Weight" 126
May 6th: "The Haunting" 127
May 7th: "It's No Fun When The Rabbit Has The Gun" 128
May 8th: "Knife Wounds" 129
May 9th: "The Closure" 130
May 10th: "Who Do I Run Too?" 131
May 11th: "I'm Offended" 132
May 12th: "The Monument" 133
May 13th: "The Substitute" 134
May 14th: "Do You Want To Learn or Be Jealous?" 135
May 15th: "Teach Me How To Swim" 136
May 16th: "This Isn't My Plan" 137
May 17th: "Bleeding On The Wire" 138
May 18th: "Are You in a Circle or a Cage?" 139
May 19th: "No Ugly Words" 140
May 20th: "God's Reputation" 141
May 21st: "The Bitter Heart" 142
May 22nd: "The Update" 143
May 23rd: "He Says, She Says, They Say" 144
May 24th: "Love From The Balcony" 145
May 25th: "Wrapped In Goodbye" 146
May 26th: "The Bulldozers" 147
May 27th: "The To-Go-Plate" 148
May 28th: "Take It or Leave It" 149
May 29th: "All Snakes Don't Hiss" 150
May 30th: "The Press Release" 151
May 31st: "From A Distance" 152

June 1st: "I'm Transitioning" 153
June 2nd: "But You Allow It" 154
June 3rd: "Overthinking It" 155
June 4th: "Making God Laugh" 156

June 5th: "It's Not From God" 157
June 6th: "They Don't Want To Be Fixed" 158
June 7th: "Don't Go Blind" 159
June 8th: "Unacceptable Behavior" 160
June 9th: "Getting Saved" 161
June 10th: "Put It In Park" 162
June 11th: "The Ugly Part" 163
June 12th: "Running Away From Yourself" 164
June 13th: "It's What I Had" 165
June 14th: "I Want Their Life" 166
June 15th: "Be Picky" 167
June 16th: "The Expose" 168
June 17th: "I Need Directions" 169
June 18th: "You Made It Before Them" 170
June 19th: "Don't Answer" 171
June 20th: "Clocks Don't Rewind" 172
June 21st: "S.O.S" 173
June 22nd: "Say Nothing, Do Nothing" 174
June 23rd: "Solid As A Rock" 175
June 24th: "Worthless To Priceless" 176
June 25th: "But What's Wrong With YOU?" 177
June 26th: "OUCH! That Hurts" 178
June 27th: "Go Stress Out Someone Else" 179
June 28th: "They Didn't Cut You" 180
June 29th: "I Grew Up" 181
June 30th: "I Don't Have It Figured Out" 182

July 1st: "Diluting Yourself" 183
July 2nd: "This is It" 184
July 3rd: "The Next Move is On You" 185
July 4th: "Cease And Desist" 186
July 5th: "I'm Breaking" 187
July 6th: "Everybody Can't Tell The Same Lie" 188
July 7th: "Full Panic Mode" 189

July 8th: "Wrong As Two Left Shoes" 190
July 9th: "Get Rid of Your Pacifier" 191
July 10th: "Access DENIED" 192
July 11th: "Lethal To My Heart" 193
July 12th: "It Ran Its Course" 194
July 13th: "Will It Ever Come?" 195
July 14th: "Repeated Lessons" 196
July 15th: "You Were Told NOT Too" 197
July 16th: "Face It: You Were Wrong" 198
July 17th: "D.E.P.R.E.S.S.I.O.N" 199
July 18th: "A Tough Decision" 200
July 19th: "Allergic To The Truth" 201
July 20th: "Walls Up (A Detached Heart)" 202
July 21st: "Trauma Bond" 203
July 22nd: "Not Defeated By The Loss" 204
July 23rd: "Forgiveness Doesn't Mean Restoration" 205
July 24th: "Living Beyond The Past" 206
July 25th: "It's Not What You Want To Hear" 207
July 26th: "Get Out Of Your Own Way" 208
July 27th: "Out of The Cocoon" 209
July 28th: "Wipe Your Tears And Face" 210
July 29th: "Perfect Time" 211
July 30th: "It's Not About What Happened To You" 212
July 31st: "You Have The Answer To The Problem" 213

August 1st: "Not Mad, Just DONE!" 214
August 2nd: "I'm Starving" 215
August 3rd: "Privacy is Power" 216
August 4th: "Is (IT) YOU?" 217
Augusts 5th: "I Didn't See It Coming" 218
August 6th: "In Recovery" 219
August 7th: "Enemy Lines" 220
August 8th: "An Override" 221
August 9th: "Stop The Temper Tantrums" 222

August 10th: "From Bad To Worse" 223
August 11th: "Intentional Silence" 224
August 12th: "Be Your Own Cheerleader" 225
August 13th: "Fight or Flight" 226
August 14th: "Get Your Priorities Straight" 227
August 15th: "The Devastation" 228
August 16th: "If The Shoe Fits Wear It" 229
August 17th: "A Bullet Dodged" 230
August 18th: "It's Everything That You Ever Wanted (In Disguised)" ... 231
August 19th: "Every Battle Isn't Public" 232
August 20th: "Life Goes On" 233
August 21st: "Thrown In The Fiery Furnace" 234
August 22nd: "The Pew Warmers" 235
August 23rd: "The Dragging Contest" 236
August 24th: "Private Integrity" 237
August 25th: "The Forgiven Ones" 238
August 26th: "Second Guessing Yourself" 239
August 27th: "Getting Even or Having Peace" 240
August 28th: "You're Giving Me A Headache" 241
August 29th: "Don't Give Fear An Audience" 242
August 30th: "Bitter Roots" 243
August 31st: "A Diamond Is Still A Diamond" 244

September 1st: "Remaining The Same" 245
September 2nd: "Growth Over Company" 246
September 3rd: "Committed To Your Ego" 247
September 4th: "Repercussions Of Bad Choices" 248
September 5th: "Mend It or End It" 249
September 6th: "You Can't Learn Their Lesson" 250
September 7th: "Complimented But Not Corrected" 251
September 8th: "Pray Before You Gossip" 252
September 9th: "I Have A Plan" 253
September 10th: "Can I Get Some Support" 254
September 11th: "Imitating The Results" 255

September 12th: "The Place of Reference" 256
September 13th: "Painting A Different Picture" 257
September 14th: "But It's Killing YOU" 258
September 15th: "Frustrated & Disappointed" 259
September 16th: "Prayers Answered in Disguised" 260
September 17th: "Same Script - Different Cast" 261
September 18th: "Being Disobedient" 262
September 19th: "Don't Let Your Eyes Keep Talking For You" 263
September 20th: "Get Off The Merry-Go-Round" 264
September 21st: "Running After What Left" 265
September 22nd: "Why Are You Putting It Back On?" 266
September 23rd: "Stop Letting Them Talk To You Into A Nightmare"..267
September 24th: "Getting Discovered" 268
September 25th: "Winning or Finishing" 269
September 26th: "When It Rains It Pours" 270
September 27th: "Teach Them Your Absence" 271
September 28th: "Let Me Explain" 272
September 29th: "Your Own Worst Enemy" 273
September 30th: "The Titanic Sunk" 274

October 1st: "This Pain I Have" 275
October 2nd: "Compete With Only You" 276
October 3rd: "I'm Distracted" 277
October 4th: "Giving Yourself Away" 278
October 5th: "Holding Your Healing Hostage" 279
October 6th: "They Prey...So You PRAY" 280
October 7th: "Blaming The Seed" 281
October 8th: "Struggling But Not Quitting" 282
October 9th: "Confront It" 283
October 10th: "Band-Aids or Stitches" 284
October 11th: "You're Acting Funny" 285
October 12th: "Test in Session: NO TALKING" 286
October 13th: "Walking Out Of The Room" 287
October 14th: "Worthless" 288

October 15th: "It's Making Me Sick!" 289
October 16th: "Drinking Poison" 290
October 17th: "Closed Eyes Don't Erase You" 291
October 18th: "Misquoted" 292
October 19th: "You Don't Like Me, and I Don't Like You" 293
October 20th: "Representing Him The Worst" 294
October 21st: "One Door" 295
October 22nd: "Butterflies Were Once Caterpillars" 296
October 23rd: "All Yellow Brick Roads Aren't The Path Home" 297
October 24th: "Don't Get Mad…Just Be Aware" 298
October 25th: "It's All I Know" 299
October 26th: "Stop Auditioning" 300
October 27th: "Discernment" 301
October 28th: "Changing Your Surroundings" 302
October 29th: "Energy Suckers" 303
October 30th: "Diapers Need To Be Changed" 304
October 31st: "New People, Same Issues" 305

November 1st: "Cutting The Umbilical Cord" 306
November 2nd: "You Have To Get Cut" 307
November 3rd: "Guard Your Garden" 308
November 4th: "The Inner – You" 309
November 5th: "Protect Your Ears" 310
November 6th: "They're Mad At You For Being Whole" 311
November 7th: "Eating From Every Plate" 312
November 8th: "Wait-Training" 313
November 9th: "Dirty Hands" 314
November 10th: "Better Is Coming" 315
November 11th: "Your Words Can Change You" 316
November 12th: "Resurrecting The Dead" 317
November 13th: "STOP Monitoring It" 318
November 14th: "The Goodbye" 319
November 15th: "But They Can't See It" 320
November 16th: "Full Attitude But Half The Facts" 321

November 17th: "Rubbing Me The Wrong Way" 322
November 18th: "Generational Curses" 323
November 19th: "Be An Elevator" 324
November 20th: "Trying To Go Back In The Shell" 325
November 21st: "God Doesn't Lose" 326
November 22nd: "Eyes Like A Lion" 327
November 23rd: "Leftovers" 328
November 24th: "Don't Put Your Gift in The Wrong Hands" 329
November 25th: "A Glossy Pit" 330
November 26th: "Committed To Your Past or Future?" 331
November 27th: "Did You Let It Go or Bury It?" 332
November 28th: "Let It Rain" 333
November 29th: "What Is Your Attitude Saying?" 334
November 30th: "Use Your Keys Wisely" 335

December 1st: "Your "YES" Doesn't Need Counsel" 336
December 2nd: "The Letdown" 337
December 3rd: "Sabotaging The Ship" 338
December 4th: "A Protected Heart" 339
December 5th: "The Stalker" 340
December 6th: "But You Got What You Wanted" 341
December 7th: "Are You Going To Be In Faith or Your Feelings?" 342
December 8th: "Their Opinion But Your Assignment" 343
December 9th: "Out of VIP" 344
December 10th: "The Obsession" 345
December 11th: "Let Them Be Mad" 346
December 12th: "Fight For It" 347
December 13th: "The Know-It-All" 348
December 14th: "Just Say NO!" 349
December 15th: "The Anointed" 350
December 16th: "Take The Medicine Please" 351
December 17th: "Control Your Own Thermostat" 352
December 18th: "Let It Play Out" 353
December 19th: "Don't Let The Accident Be Your Choice!" 354

December 20th: "The Power of Stepping Away" 355
December 21st: "Grown Ups" 356
December 22nd: "Biting Your Tongue" 357
December 23rd: "Expecting YOU From Other Folks" 358
December 24th: "Stinkin' Thinkin'" 359
December 25th: "The Runaway" 360
December 26th: "Change Your Flat Tire" 361
December 27th: "Sticks & Stones" 362
December 28th: "Who's Really With Me?" 363
December 29th: "Own Your Part" 364
December 30th: "It Could've Been You" 365
December 31st: "Which One: Surgery or Pain Killers?" 366

About the Author 367

PREFACE

IN THE MORNING

In the morning as I rise,

May I meet you as the sun cracks the sky

May my ears stay open to hear your sweetest voice

So that I am prepared to meet hope throughout the day

Trusting that you have gone before me and paved my way

In the morning as I rise,

May I posture myself with gratefulness as I notice the evidence of being kept alive

In the morning as I rise

I'll seek you first, knowing that only you shall quench my every thirst

Oh Lord, in the morning as I rise

May I listen for your sweetest voice

Knowing that your word will guide me through life's course.

Oh Lord, in the morning as I rise

May I take notice of your glory filled in the majestic skies

Oh Lord, in the morning as I rise

I shall posture myself with gratefulness as I notice the evidence of you keeping me alive

In the morning as I rise

May the new dawning quicken me to recall that from dust to dawn

It is your sovereignty that has surrounded me and allowed nothing through the night to bring me harm

Even through the toils and snares of yesterday

May the new dawning quicken me to recall that from dust to dawn

It is your sovereignty that woke me on purpose for your divine purpose

Oh Lord,

In the morning as I rise

I am grateful that you have kept me alive.

There's something about the sun rising that reminds a believer that the night sky has passed.

All things are made anew and a new opportunity for opportunities shall spring forth

The day sky brings an awakening reminder of the evidence of God's goodness.

Arise and seek his Glory morning after morning

Author/Spoken Word Vessel
Shannon Talley

INTRODUCTION

Night after night with heavy thoughts of hurt and sadness. She began to fill her bed with pillow-soaked tears. Never did she think she would see the morning.

It was until she lost everything that she began to find herself. She was no longer mourning in despair but discovering the power behind her tears that fell.

Although her life the past couple of years wasn't a crystal staircase, she learned that weeping may endure for the night, but joy will come in the morning.

And it was then that she began to rise and embrace the dawn.

She is Travasa Holloway of TNHB Inspirations.

DEVOTIONALS

365 DAYS OF TNHB INSPIRATIONS

JANUARY 1ST

"UNSTOPPABLE"

Growing up, you would hear adults say, "That kid is hardheaded." Meaning he or she didn't listen.

Ironically, that's how a lot of folks are today. They know better, but they don't do better.

See, God has shown you repeatedly; if you do it your way, "that" will be the outcome. But if you trust in His way, everything will be just fine. (Proverbs 3:5)

Remember, God's plans are entirely UNSTOPPABLE. You can try to fight against them if you want to, but they will succeed!!! (Proverbs 19:21)

"The LORD's plans stand firm forever; his intentions can never be shaken. (Psalm 33:11)

In The Morning

_____

_____

_____

_____

_____

_____

_____

_____

_____

JANUARY 2ND

"FOR THE RIGHT REASONS"

Have you ever felt like problems are coming from the North, South, East, and West? And before you know it, everything falls apart.

See your hardships, heartbreak, and trials might be the worst thing that you're going through. BUT GOD!!!! (James 1:2)

Remember, everything that seems to be going wrong - is actually working for the RIGHT reasons.

"As for you, you meant evil against me, but God meant it for good in order to bring about this present result," (Genesis 50:20)

In The Morning

_____

_____

_____

_____

_____

_____

_____

_____

_____

_____

_____

_____

_____

JANUARY 3ʳᴰ

"BUT THE YEAR CHANGED"

It's the third day of the new year. Some folks made New Year's resolutions and have decided to stick to what they made promises to. At the same time, others chose to break them already. The question is: Which have you done?

See, there is no judgment either way. But you can't expect to change because the new year has arrived automatically.

Remember, things don't change because the year changed. If you want to see a difference, you will have to do the work and make it change.

"In all labour, there is profit: but the talk of the lips *tendeth* only to penury." (Proverbs 14:23)

IN THE MORNING

JANUARY 4TH

"DON'T FORFEIT WHAT HAS BEEN PURPOSED"

Fed up.

Irritated.

Sick and Tired.

If that's YOU, you're not alone.

It's very common to get inflamed with your anointing. And asking the question, "What do I do?"

Simple, hold your head back up and shake it off. Is it painful? YES! But though He slays you. YET, you STILL must trust HIM!!!! (Job 13:15)

Remember, don't let the frustration forfeit what has been PURPOSED. If you do, you allow the pain in the moment to cause you to give up. And you're a winner.

There will be a LESSON and a REWARD in the end. AND YOU WIN!!!!!!!!!!!!

"No temptation has overtaken you except what is common to mankind. And God is faithful; He will not let you be tempted beyond what you can bear. But when you are tempted, He will also provide a way out so that you can endure it." (1 Corinthians 10:13)

In The Morning

_____

_____

_____

_____

JANUARY 5TH

"STOP TRYING TO STEAL THE PEN"

"I want it to go this way." "We are planning this." "I have everything all worked out."

Sound familiar?

See, it's easy to sit and plan on what and how you think your story is going to be played out. But the fact is, you can make all the plans you want to make, but it's the Lord's purpose and will that will ALWAYS prevail. (Proverbs 19:21)

Remember, God is writing your story, NOT YOU!!!! STOP trying to steal the pen!

"Looking unto Jesus, the author and finisher of *our* faith," (Hebrews 12:2)

IN THE MORNING

_____
_____
_____
_____
_____
_____
_____
_____
_____
_____
_____

JANUARY 6TH

"STOP ASKING BLIND PEOPLE TO PROOFREAD YOUR VISION"

You wrote the vision and ran with it. (Habakkuk 2:2) So why do you keep asking other folks for their opinion?

It's time to stop getting a co-signer for the gift that God has placed inside of you. Folks will always have something to say. It doesn't matter if they like it. But it does matter if you love it and want to do it.

Remember, stop asking blind people to proofread your vision.

"But you, take courage! Do not let your hands be weak, for your work shall be rewarded." (2 Chronicles 15:7)

In The Morning

_____

_____

_____

_____

_____

_____

_____

_____

_____

_____

_____

_____

JANUARY 7TH

"BUT IT'S NOT ATTRACTIVE"

"The grass is not always greener on the other side." How many of you have heard that saying before? Now how many of you have gone on the other side, only to discover the grass was fake?

See, things that glitter often look attractive. But just because it glitters doesn't mean it's gold. Some things are bright and shiny, but rotten in the core.

Always be careful of jumping ship when you don't know what you might jump into. Your assigned place may not be what you THINK is attractive. But don't leave it for what you *think* is better either.

Stay where Grace covers you.

"Nevertheless, each person should live as a believer in whatever situation the Lord has assigned to them, just as God has called them." (1 Corinthians 7:17)

IN THE MORNING

_____

_____

_____

_____

_____

_____

_____

_____

JANUARY 8TH

"THE APOLOGY YOU'LL NEVER GET"

When you've been done wrong, it hurts. And it's a knee-jerk reaction to want and expect an apology afterward. But sometimes, that's not what you're going to get.

See, there comes a time that you have to move on and simply forgive. Even if that means you will never get your "sorry."

Remember, you have to accept the apology that you will never get from protecting that peace that your heart and anointing desires.

"See to it that no one falls short of the grace of God and that no bitter root grows up to cause trouble and defile many." (Hebrews 12:15)

"Instead, be kind to each other, tenderhearted, forgiving one another, just as God through Christ has forgiven you." (Ephesians 4:32)

In The Morning

_____

_____

_____

_____

_____

_____

_____

JANUARY 9TH

"DIGGING UP DOUBT"

Have you ever felt like you've done everything you're supposed to do but still feel forgotten about by God?

See, it's easy to feel loved by Him when everything is going well. But can you still praise and trust in Him when things get weary?

Remember, what you plant in faith, you can't dig back up with doubt.

"But when you ask, you must believe and not doubt, because the one who doubts is like a wave of the sea, blown and tossed by the wind." (James 1:6)

In The Morning

JANUARY 10TH

"STEP OUT OF THE RACE"

When you're in a race, you want to win. But sometimes, folks get caught up worrying about what the other competitors are doing. And they shouldn't.

See, you must stay focused on your prize. You are not in this to see how he or she is competing. So it doesn't matter how they are running or training. Just focus on yourself, and YOU WILL WIN!

Remember, step out of the race you THINK you're in, and run your lane!!!!

"I have fought the good fight, I have finished the race, I have kept the faith." (2 Timothy 4:7)

In The Morning

_____

_____

_____

_____

_____

_____

_____

_____

_____

_____

_____

_____

JANUARY 11TH

"LIKE HUSKS FALLING OFF CORN"

In life, some things are no longer needed and serve you no purpose. Meaning, it's time to let it go!

Whether it's a toxic relationship or a friendship that's draining, a job that's going nowhere, or clothes that you know you'll never get into again. LET IT GO!!!

Just as a husk falls off of corn, you, too, must let go of what shouldn't remain any longer!

"Remember not the former things, nor consider the things of old. Behold, I am doing a new thing; now it springs forth, do you not perceive it? I will make a way in the wilderness and rivers in the desert." (Isaiah 43:18-19)

IN THE MORNING

_____
_____
_____
_____
_____
_____
_____
_____
_____
_____
_____
_____
_____

JANUARY 12TH

"IT'S YOUR PATH"

Obstacles are nothing but things that block and prevent progress. So how many of you have obstacles in your life currently?

See, you must learn how to stop focusing on the obstacles and see how they will help in your advancement. Because without the struggles and hardships, you wouldn't know what you could endure. (James 1:12)

Remember, obstacles are not there to block your path. They ARE YOUR PATH!

"Dear brothers and sisters, when troubles come your way, consider it an opportunity for great joy. For you know that when your faith is tested, your endurance has a chance to grow. So let it grow, for when your endurance is fully developed, you will be perfect and complete, needing nothing." (James 1:2-4)

In The Morning

_____

_____

_____

_____

_____

_____

_____

_____

JANUARY 13TH

TALK IS CHEAP! "BUT THE CONSEQUENCES ARE EXPENSIVE"

"Talk is cheap." How many of you have heard that phrase before?

See, sometimes talking too much can get you in trouble. But those who guard their mouth will preserve their life from the repercussions from the tongue. (Proverbs 13:3)

Remember, talk is cheap - but the consequences can be very expensive!

"The mouths of fools are their ruin; they trap themselves with their lips." (Proverbs 18:7)

In The Morning

_____
_____
_____
_____
_____
_____
_____
_____
_____
_____
_____
_____
_____

JANUARY 14TH

"SEND THEM A THANK YOU CARD"

They hurt you and meant to, and it's because of what they did; you don't even trust them now. How many can relate?

Unfortunately, that's a typical story for many. But no longer should you feel ashamed or sad.

Because what they meant for evil, God means for your good. (Genesis 50:20) (Romans 8:28) (Romans 12:19)

Remember, the only thing you need to do is say, Thank You!

"May the LORD judge between you and me. And may the LORD avenge the wrongs you have done to me, but my hand will not touch you." (1 Samuel 24:12)

In The Morning

_____
_____
_____
_____
_____
_____
_____
_____
_____
_____
_____
_____

JANUARY 15TH

"A BAD LANDING"

Hot-headed. Frantic. Raging. Deranged. Sound familiar? See, that's how some folks act when they go into a rage. The question is: Does that describe YOU?

Remember, the same people who fly into a rage always make a bad landing.

KEEP CALM!!!!!!

"Understand this, my dear brothers and sisters: You must all be quick to listen, slow to speak, and slow to get angry. Human anger does not produce the righteousness God desires." (James 1:19-20)

In The Morning

_____
_____
_____
_____
_____
_____
_____
_____
_____
_____
_____
_____
_____
_____

JANUARY 16TH

"WAITING FOR THE SNAILS TO COME INTO THE ARK"

Patience is a virtue. That's a saying that we all have heard before. But how many of you have patience?

See, patience is the capacity to accept or tolerate delay. Although you want it now - RIGHT NOW. That doesn't mean that you're going to get it.

Remember, Noah had to gather all the animals into the Ark. Patience is Noah waiting for the snails to come in. (Genesis 6:19-21)

It's time to wait for the Lord and be of good courage. His Word and promises for your life are true!!!! (Psalm 27:14) & (Jeremiah 29:11)

"Wait for the LORD and keep His way, and He will raise you up to inherit the land." (Psalm 37:34)

IN THE MORNING

_____
_____
_____
_____
_____
_____
_____
_____
_____

JANUARY 17TH

"NOISE MAKER"

"I go to church every Sunday."

"I know what the "good book" says."

"I'm a Christian."

See, you can say and do many things, but if it doesn't line up with your walk. What does it mean?

Remember, you can quote scriptures all day and back to back. But when your lifestyle says and does the opposite, you're just a noisemaker.

"If someone claims, "I know God," but doesn't obey God's commandments, that person is a liar and is not living in the truth." (1 John 2:4)

"Therefore, whoever knows the right thing to do, yet fails to do it, is guilty of sin." (James 4:17)

In The Morning

_____
_____
_____
_____
_____
_____
_____
_____

JANUARY 18TH

"SNOOZE YOU LOSE"

Have you ever been the reason something didn't work out? See, everything that's a delay isn't the devil's fault. Often, the problem, hindrance, and lack of progress in your life are because of YOU!!!

So if you're looking for someone to blame, look in the mirror.

Remember, you snooze, you lose!

"The soul of the sluggard craves and gets nothing, while the soul of the diligent is richly supplied." (Proverbs 13:4)

In The Morning

_____

_____

_____

_____

_____

_____

_____

_____

_____

_____

_____

_____

_____

_____

_____

JANUARY 19TH

"IT'S WHAT YOU NEED"

Have you ever wanted something so badly that you were devastated when you didn't get it?

See, it's okay to want what you want. But just because you want it doesn't mean God wants it for you.

Remember, there are some situations when not getting what you want is what you need.

"God has blocked my way so I cannot move." (Job 19:8)

In The Morning

_____
_____
_____
_____
_____
_____
_____
_____
_____
_____
_____
_____
_____
_____
_____
_____
_____

JANUARY 20ᵀᴴ

"WHAT HURT YOU, DOESN'T HAVE TO HAUNT YOU"

Does it feel good to get hurt? NO!
Will you get through it? YES!

See, some folks will replay the bad parts of their life over and over. And before they know it, the past begins to haunt them.

Remember, your healing is now, and what hurt you doesn't have to haunt you.

"For I will be merciful toward their iniquities, and I will remember their sins no more." (Hebrews 8:12)

In The Morning

_____
_____
_____
_____
_____
_____
_____
_____
_____
_____
_____
_____

JANUARY 21ST

"THE VILLAIN"

Some people in this world are just cold-hearted. And sometimes, it's the ones closest to you that hurt you the most.

I get it! You're hurt, angry, and want revenge. But it's not for you to vindicate. (Hebrews 10:30)

The truth is, the Lord WILL handle your foes and avenge the wrongs that have been done to you. But your hand will NOT touch them. (1 Samuel 24:12)

Remember, you don't have to make your enemies a villain and tell everyone what they did. Just say, "Thank you." And Let God handle what He has promised.

"Do not avenge yourselves, beloved, but leave room for God's wrath. For it is written: "Vengeance is Mine; I will repay, says the Lord." (Romans 12:19)

In The Morning

_____
_____
_____
_____
_____
_____
_____
_____
_____
_____

JANUARY 22ND

"TRAINED TO COMPLAIN"

Have you ever had these complaints?

"I don't like it here."

"They get on my nerves."

"I'm so unhappy."

"I want to go."

See, complaining is something that's almost a knee-jerk reaction to some folks. But be careful because what you say has power. (Proverbs 18:21)

Remember, don't be trained to complain about people, places, and things. YES! You don't like your situation. But instead of complaining, praise instead. It's a matter of FAITH, not feelings.

"And don't complain as some of them did and were killed by the destroyer." (1 Corinthians 10:10)

"Give thanks in all circumstances; for this is the will of God in Christ Jesus for you." (1 Thessalonians 5:18)

In The Morning

_____
_____
_____
_____
_____
_____

JANUARY 23ᴿᴰ

"PLEADING MY CASE"

Have you ever begged and tried to reason with someone to hear you out, but their mind was made up?

See, it's time to stop pleading your case. The plots and schemes won't work either. God is saying," Give it to me." (Psalm 55:22)

If they want to go, let them. You can't be so quick to pick chickens when God is trying to give you an eagle.

"They went out from us, but they did not really belong to us. For if they had belonged to us, they would have remained with us; but their going showed that none of them belonged to us." (1 John 2:19)

In The Morning

JANUARY 24TH

"IT'S OKAY TO BE THE TORTOISE"

It's taking too long. It seems as if you will never get there. Everyone else is getting ahead, and you're still at the same starting point. Sound familiar?

Today, tap yourself and say, "It doesn't matter if I'm the tortoise."

In other words, whether you're the tortoise or the hare. You're going to get there when YOU get there. Who cares what your neighbor is doing. YOU just keep pressing forward! (1 Corinthians 9:24)

Remember, your speed doesn't matter. Forward IS forward!

"I press on toward the goal for the prize of the upward call of God in Christ Jesus." (Philippians 3:14)

In The Morning

_____
_____
_____
_____
_____
_____
_____
_____
_____
_____
_____

JANUARY 25TH

"APPRECIATION DAY"

Your life is busy. You have kids now. You're married. A career woman. A businessman. Entrepreneur. To sum it up, you have a lot going on.

YES! Your calendar is booked to the max. But you can never be too busy to appreciate who and what you have.

Remember, choose to make time to have your own "Appreciation Day." Because every day is not promised, and what's taken for granted will soon be taken away. (Matthew 13:12)

"Be joyful always; pray continually; give thanks in all circumstances, for this is God's will for you in Christ Jesus. (1 Thessalonians 5:16-18)

In The Morning

_____
_____
_____
_____
_____
_____
_____
_____
_____
_____
_____
_____

JANUARY 26TH

"STOP THE ADVICE & AUDIENCE"

You're hurt. You vent, cry, and spill your feelings. Now you have an audience that knows all about what you're going through. And before you know it, the whole town, city, and state know your heartbreak and trials. Sound familiar?

Today is the day that you learn to guard your mouth. YES! You can have confidants. But you must be careful who you confide in. (Proverbs 21:23)

Remember, some critical things in your life don't need advice or an audience. Some people want to MIND your business to MINE your business. (Bishop L. Spenser Smith)

"Do not rely on a friend; do not trust in a companion. Seal the doors of your mouth from her who lies in your arms." (Micah 7:5)

In The Morning

_____
_____
_____
_____
_____
_____
_____
_____
_____
_____

JANUARY 27ᵀᴴ

"PUT YOUR FENCE UP"

They keep picking, hitting, throwing rocks, and hiding their hands. Now you want to retaliate. Sound familiar?

See, it's time to put your fence up. Meaning, put on the spiritual armor of God. (Ephesians 6:10-18)

The enemy knows what they're doing. Their goal is to get you to fall for their schemes and tricks. But the devil is a lie!!!

Remember, safety is a fence. So put it up.

"The LORD will fight for you; you need only to be still." (Exodus 14:14)

In The Morning

_____
_____
_____
_____
_____
_____
_____
_____
_____
_____
_____
_____
_____
_____

JANUARY 28TH

"I NEED A NEW PENCIL"

A young lady once kept throwing out no. 2 pencils after the wood would cover the lead. She did this because she said they were no good. Little did she know, it just needs to be sharpened.

Today, tap yourself and say, "I just need to be sharpened."

See, we think that we're no good a lot of times because we can't endure the pain of trials in life. But that's a lie! (Philippians 4:13)

Remember, when sharpening a pencil, there are layers being peeled back. The newness begins, and it's painfully sharpened for you to make a point!

"Using a dull ax requires great strength, so sharpen the blade. That's the value of wisdom; it helps you succeed." (Ecclesiastes 10:10)

In The Morning

_____
_____
_____
_____
_____
_____
_____
_____
_____

JANUARY 29TH

"PRAYER WARRIOR VS. PRAYER WORRIER"

"I'm a warrior." "I'm a fighter." "I'm victorious." But as soon as trouble and trials hit, you're the first to panic and fall out to the floor. Now surely that isn't you, is it?

Today is the day you define whether you're going to be a "Warrior" or a "Worrier."

The truth is, God doesn't give you a spirit of fear, so what are you terrified of? (2 Timothy 1:7)

Remember, when trouble hits, become a "PRAYER WARRIOR," not a worrier.

"Do not be anxious about anything, but in everything by prayer and supplication with thanksgiving let your requests be made known to God. And the peace of God, which surpasses all understanding, will guard your hearts and your minds in Christ Jesus." (Philippians 4:6-7)

In The Morning

_____
_____
_____
_____
_____
_____
_____
_____

JANUARY 30TH

"THE ALLIGATOR ON THE LADDER"

"The enemy is blocking me from moving forward."

"My boss won't advance me."

"They keep holding me back."

Sound familiar?

See, your delay isn't always others' fault. At some point, YOU have to acknowledge your actions as well.

Remember, if an alligator was climbing a ladder, his mouth would be blocking him from going up. So don't YOU be that alligator!

"The LORD says, "I will guide you along the best pathway for your life. I will advise you and watch over you." (Psalm 32:8)

IN THE MORNING

_____
_____
_____
_____
_____
_____
_____
_____
_____
_____
_____
_____

JANUARY 31ST

"DIGGING BACK UP YOUR SEED"

When you sow a seed, you're putting it into the ground to await your harvest.

Now everyone sows seeds in various ways. But at the end of the day, what you sow will eventually sprout.

Remember, don't get to tripping and dig up your seed because of how others are dealing with you.

In the end, it's God that will reward YOU, not folks! (Galatians 6:9)

"Do not be deceived: God is not mocked, for whatever one sows, that will he also reap." (Galatians 6:7)

In The Morning

FEBRUARY 1ST

"KEEPING THE INFECTION FROM SPREADING"

When you get sick, sometimes you get what is commonly known as an infection. Whether it's bacterial or viral, it is a top priority once in your system to get it out.

See, folks often cry and get enraged because something or someone has been cut off from them.

But like anything that has been infected, God will remove it to keep it from spreading.

"He heals the brokenhearted and binds up their wounds." (Psalm 147:3)

In The Morning

_____
_____
_____
_____
_____
_____
_____
_____
_____
_____
_____
_____
_____

FEBRUARY 2ND

"CANCEL YOUR SUBSCRIPTION"

Have you ever found yourself entangled with drama, gossipers, or haters?

See, chaos and discord can be too much to handle. But there is something that you can do about it.

It's simple, cancel your subscription to all the negativity and unwanted press.

Remember, happiness is a choice, and it's yours to make!

"A joyful heart is good medicine, but a crushed spirit dries up the bones." (Proverbs 17:22)

In The Morning

_____
_____
_____
_____
_____
_____
_____
_____
_____
_____
_____
_____
_____
_____

FEBRUARY 3ᴿᴰ

"BUT I'M PART-TIME"

Full time means you get the whole of someone's availability. Part-time means a part of the availability. So, ask yourself how much availability are you giving God?

I get it. You're irritated and frustrated and want God to move and answer your problems now. But God doesn't work like that.

See, here is the thing, the irritation, frustration, and attitude that you're feeling shouldn't be directed at God, for He says that He will never leave nor forsake you. He's always there. But are YOU? (Deuteronomy 31:6)

Remember, you can't expect a full-time God in a part-time relationship.

"Draw near to God and He will draw near to you." (Hebrews 4:8)

In The Morning

FEBRUARY 4TH

"GROW IN THE DIRT"

"Abandoned"

"Mishandled"

"Mistreated"

"Left to die."

Sound familiar?

I get it, it's not right, and it's not fair. So what do you do? YOU GROW!!!!

See, what they did was wrong, but it's for God to handle, not you. (Exodus 14:13-14)

Remember, it's time to grow from the dirt you were left in, and let God handle those who put you there.

"They are like trees planted along a riverbank, with roots that reach deep into the water. Such trees are not bothered by the heat or worried by long months of drought. Their leaves stay green, and they never stop producing fruit." (Jeremiah 17:8)

In The Morning

_____

_____

_____

_____

_____

_____

_____

FEBRUARY 5TH

"THE RED MUSCLE IN YOUR MOUTH"

When you're heated, angry, or mad, it can cause your tongue to do significant damage.

See, it's okay to be upset, but silence is a source of great strength. (Lao Tzu)

Remember, just hush until you heal, let the red muscle (tongue) in your mouth be still.

My dear brothers and sisters, take note of this: Everyone should be quick to listen, slow to speak, and slow to become angry, (James 1:19)

In The Morning

_____
_____
_____
_____
_____
_____
_____
_____
_____
_____
_____
_____
_____
_____

FEBRUARY 6TH

"THE CONDITIONS HAVE CHANGED"

Faith is the assurance of things hoped for, the conviction of things not seen. Now ask yourself: Do you have faith? (Hebrews 11:1)

See, things are going to happen in life that will be overwhelming. But that doesn't mean you throw in the towel and give up?

It's at that point when you must continue to press forward, no matter what the circumstance is. (Philippians 3:14)

Remember, your confession must remain consistent when it comes to your faith, even when the conditions shift.

"For we walk by faith, not by sight." (2 Corinthians 5:7)

In The Morning

FEBRUARY 7TH

"YOU DIDN'T FAIL, YOU FELL"

Fail is being unsuccessful in achieving one's goal. Fell is the past tense of fall in which a person can fall down a flight of stairs.

See, sometimes things don't work the way you want, but it doesn't mean it's over. Because your fall only becomes your failure if you stay down.

Remember, falling can be by chance, but failure is by choice.

So get back up and continue your work!

"For the righteous falls seven times and rises again," (Proverbs 24:16)

IN THE MORNING

_____
_____
_____
_____
_____
_____
_____
_____
_____
_____
_____
_____
_____

FEBRUARY 8TH

"RAGGEDY TO ROYALTY"

"Abandonment"

"Danger"

"Isolation"

"Worthlessness"

Sound Familiar?

See, the enemy wants you to believe that you'll never get out of the dark place you're in right now. But he's a lie!!!!!

It's time to be like David and encourage yourself. He had opposition but went from raggedy to royalty. (1 Samuel 30:6) (1 Samuel 5, 16 & 1 Samuel 19)

Remember, activate your faith, and God will turn your tragedy into triumph. You're not forgotten, but you are favored!

"But thanks *be* to God, the *One* always leading us in triumph in Christ," (2 Corinthians 2:14)

In The Morning

___
___
___
___
___
___
___
___

FEBRUARY 9TH

"KEEP READING"

Have things ever been so bad that you just wanted to give up? See, sometimes life will have you feel like you don't know what to do. But the truth is this isn't the first time you felt like this, and it won't be the last.

The same God that rescued you before will do it again! (Psalm 37:39)

Remember, your story isn't over just because you're in a lousy chapter. Keep reading (living).

"You came to my rescue, Lord, and saved my life." (Lamentations 3:58)

IN THE MORNING

_____

_____

_____

_____

_____

_____

_____

_____

_____

_____

FEBRUARY 10TH

"BUT YOU STEPPED ON THEM THOUGH"

Because it didn't come dressed the way you wanted, you think it isn't good enough.

Surely that's doesn't describe you, does it?

See, you can't be so quick to throw out what you think is trash because it's packaged differently.

Remember, stop stepping on the person God sent to bless you, trying to get to another that won't even help you at all.

"Do not judge by appearances, but judge with right judgment." (John 7:24)

In The Morning

FEBRUARY 11ᵀᴴ

"AT THE BREAKING POINT"

When you're at a breaking point, that's when things are critical. Why? Because you're at the mark that you've been stressed to your limits.

The question is: Are you at that point?

See, you might be getting attacked from every side. But the enemy wouldn't be attacking if something precious wasn't inside of YOU.

The truth is, thieves don't break into empty houses. YOU have a purpose!

Remember, your BREAKTHROUGH is on the other side of your breaking point.

"We are pressed on every side by troubles, but we are not crushed. We are perplexed, but not driven to despair. We are hunted down, but never abandoned by God. We get knocked down, but we are not destroyed." (2 Corinthians 4:8-9)

In The Morning

_____

_____

_____

_____

_____

_____

_____

FEBRUARY 12TH

"PUT THEM ON YOUR PRAYER LIST"

Have you ever been quick to put others down?

See, it's easy to look at someone else's life and say what you would do. But you're not them, nor do you know the hell that they're enduring.

Remember, instead of putting them down, put them on your prayer list!

"Brothers and sisters, do not slander one another. Anyone who speaks against a brother or sister or judges them speaks against the law and judges it. When you judge the law, you are not keeping it, but sitting in judgment on it. There is only one Lawgiver and Judge, the one who is able to save and destroy. But you--who are you to judge your neighbor?" (James 4:11-12)

In The Morning

_____

_____

_____

_____

_____

_____

_____

_____

_____

_____

FEBRUARY 13TH

"JUST DON'T"

You're ready to throw in the towel and surrender. Sound familiar? See, when life gets tough, folks get tired. But just because you're tired doesn't mean you quit.

Remember, you might feel like giving up, JUST DON'T!

"Let us not grow weary in well-doing, for in due time we will reap a harvest if we do not give up." (Galatians 6:9)

IN THE MORNING

FEBRUARY 14TH

"I'M TOO DISAPPOINTED"

Disappointed folks have a sense of sadness or displeasure by the nonfulfillment of their hopes. The question is: Does that describe you?

See, you can't allow the disappointment about what hasn't happened to stop you from believing that it will.

The truth is, just because God hasn't done it yet, doesn't mean He won't.

Remember, His time NOT yours!!!!

"For still the vision awaits its appointed time; it hastens to the end—it will not lie. If it seems slow, wait for it; it will surely come; it will not delay." (Habakkuk 2:3)

IN THE MORNING

_____
_____
_____
_____
_____
_____
_____
_____
_____
_____
_____

FEBRUARY 15TH

"EVERYTHING IS WORKING AGAINST ME"

-Job

-Work

-Kids

-Relationships

-Family

And they're all under attack. Sound familiar?

See, life can test you to make you think everything is coming against you. But it's not. (James 1:2-4)

Remember, your trials are working for your good!

"And we know that God causes all things to work together for good to those who love God, to those who are called according to His purpose." (Romans 8:28)

In The Morning

_____

_____

_____

_____

_____

_____

_____

_____

FEBRUARY 16TH

"I HAVE A PROBLEM"

You're sitting there stressing about a problem that life has thrown you. Sound familiar?

See, everyone has something that they're dealing with. Now the size of what you're going through versus someone else might be different. But the fact remains, WE all have problems.

Remember, God already had a solution before there was a problem.

So STOP fretting. IT IS WELL!

"Fear not, for I am with you; be not dismayed, for I am your God; I will strengthen you, I will help you, I will uphold you with my righteous right hand." (Isaiah 41:10)

In The Morning

_____
_____
_____
_____
_____
_____
_____
_____
_____
_____
_____
_____

FEBRUARY 17TH

"YOU'RE ATTACKING ME"

Have you ever felt attacked? And it's because someone is telling you what you NEED to hear.

See, accountability is taking responsibility for your actions. And sometimes, folks don't want to hear what they already know.

Remember, accountability will feel like an attack if you're not ready to acknowledge your behavior.

"So be careful how you live. Don't live like fools, but like those who are wise." (Ephesians 5:15)

In The Morning

FEBRUARY 18TH

"REMEMBER, GOD FORGIVES YOU"

Has someone wronged you, and now they want forgiveness? But you can't forgive them.

See, it's common to hold resentment when someone has hurt you, but it comes at a cost when you do. And it's not to them, but YOU.

Remember, you must forgive others as God forgives YOU.

"But if you do not forgive others, then your Father will not forgive your transgressions." (Matthew 6:15)

In The Morning

FEBRUARY 19TH

"IF ONLY THE MOUTH WAS CLOSED"

Because you don't believe in yourself, you speak negatively. Now surely that isn't YOU, is it?

See, the inner critic inside can talk you out of your blessing. And the tongue has power, either you speak life or death, but the choice is YOURS. (Proverbs 18:21)

So if it seems as if the "doors of life" are constantly being shut, it could be that you can't keep your mouth closed.

Remember, sometimes your harvest will depend on you hushing for a season!

"From the fruit of a person's mouth his stomach is satisfied; he is filled with the product of his lips." (Proverbs 18:20)

In The Morning

FEBRUARY 20TH

"IT'S OKAY TO SAY NO"

The word "no" is such a small saying, yet many folks have a real problem with it. Why a problem? Because it is often associated with being rude or selfish.

See, contrary to popular belief, "no" isn't a bad thing. Sometimes you have to say it because you know your worth and value. And it's okay to stand up for your beliefs.

Remember, "NO" isn't a negative word. So permit yourself to say it!

"Stand your ground, putting on the belt of truth and the body armor of God's righteousness." (Ephesians 6:14)

In The Morning

FEBRUARY 21ST

"EYES FIXED ON GOD"

When the struggles of life come, and oh yes, you'd better believe they will come, the number one focus must be to rely on truth. And truth can be challenging to uncover in this world, but God's promises are always true. (1 Corinthians 1:9)

See, it's easy to focus your attention on the trials at hand. But God is bigger than anything that you will face. (Jeremiah 32:27)

Remember, you can't see God if you fix your eyes only on trouble.

"I have told you all this so that you may have peace in me. Here on earth you will have many trials and sorrows. But take heart, because I have overcome the world." (John 16:33)

In The Morning

_____
_____
_____
_____
_____
_____
_____
_____
_____
_____
_____
_____

FEBRUARY 22ND

"PAIN, NOT THE PREFERRED TEACHER"

There is no one living that hasn't dealt with an experience of pain. And yes, it's no fun, it comes with all unwanted emotions, but it can be a blessing in disguise.

See, your pain can push you to the next level. It will cause you to be uncomfortable, but it will also show you what you're really made of.

Remember, pain may not be your preferred teacher, but it is the most effective one!

"Yet what we suffer now is nothing compared to the glory he will reveal to us later." (Romans 8:18)

In The Morning

FEBRUARY 23ᴿᴰ

"5+4=9"

Have you ever been in a heated argument? And it's because your point of view was different from someone else's.

See, everyone has their way of thinking and their perspective. It doesn't mean they're wrong. It just means their way of looking at things is different from yours.

5+4=9, but so does 7+2. Neither is wrong. They are just two different ways of getting to the number.

Remember, learn to respect others' opinions and their way of thinking.

"Love one another warmly as Christians and be eager to show respect for one another." (Romans 12:10)

In The Morning

_____
_____
_____
_____
_____
_____
_____
_____
_____
_____

FEBRUARY 24ᵀᴴ

"THE GIFT ISN'T FOR EVERYBODY"

God has given everyone unique abilities, gifts, and talents. The question is, are you true to yours?

See, using your gifts and talents for God's purpose involves your personal vision and understanding. And everyone isn't going to like nor understand what you've been called to do.

But God has entrusted you, and it's your responsibility to live by trust according to His will and desire.

Remember, don't quit when your gift is rejected because your gift is not for everybody.

"For God's gifts and His call are irrevocable." (Romans 11:29)

In The Morning

FEBRUARY 25TH

"YOU OWE YOURSELF AN APOLOGY"

Have you ever been in a situation that wasn't your fault? But you ended up blaming yourself anyways.

See, the inner critic packs a powerful punch. And there is a difference between taking responsibility and holding others accountable.

It's time to give yourself an apology for carrying the weight that wasn't yours to carry.

"For we must all appear before the judgment seat of Christ, so that each of us may receive what is due us for the things done while in the body, whether good or bad." (2 Corinthians 5:10)

In The Morning

_____
_____
_____
_____
_____
_____
_____
_____
_____
_____
_____
_____

FEBRUARY 26TH

"NO THANK YOU"

When someone invites you to an event, it's a polite thing to say yes. But what happens when you know you shouldn't go?

See, it can be difficult to say no. But all invitations don't have to be accepted. Your time and energy are priceless.

Remember, some invitations aren't blessings. You must know when to say thank you, but NO THANK YOU!

"Therefore, beloved, since you already know these things, be on your guard so that you will not be carried away by the error of the lawless and fall from your secure standing." (2 Peter 3:17)

In The Morning

_____
_____
_____
_____
_____
_____
_____
_____
_____
_____
_____
_____
_____

FEBRUARY 27ᵀᴴ

"YOU'RE NOT FINISHED"

Have you ever failed or made a mistake? And the pain of it was too much to bear.

See, no one wants to fail. It's unpleasant and uncomfortable. But through your errors, you will learn a lot, which will make you wiser.

Remember, just because you failed doesn't mean you're finished. God will use you despite your insufficiencies.

"For I can do everything through Christ, who gives me strength." (Philippians 4:13)

In The Morning

_____
_____
_____
_____
_____
_____
_____
_____
_____
_____
_____
_____

FEBRUARY 28TH

"THE LIONS YOU FACE"

We all face "lions" in our lives. Whether it be fears, feelings, or difficult situations – they exist.

The question is, what do you do when YOU encounter them?

See, you have power, dominion, and authority. And although it might FEEL like you're going to be eaten alive, rest assure you won't! (Luke 10:19) (Psalm 8:6)

Remember, Daniel, David, and Samson all faced lions but dealt with them according to their purpose. (Daniel 6:12-28) (1 Samuel 17:34-36) (Judges 14:5-6)

What am I saying?

YOU have a purpose, and now it's time to face your "lions."

"The LORD is my light and my salvation— so why should I be afraid? The LORD is my fortress, protecting me from danger, so why should I tremble?" (Psalm 27:1)

In The Morning

MARCH 1ST

"HURT HAPPENS"

Life can be a roller-coaster ride of emotions. It's full of ups and downs and filled with an array of unexpected surprises. The question is, how do you handle hurt when encountered?

See, God doesn't say you will hurt and have pain; now figure it out on your own. NO!

He says, FEAR NOT, for I am with YOU; be not dismayed, for I am your God. (Isaiah 41:10)

Remember, hurt is going to happen, but so does healing!!!

"Nevertheless, I will bring health and healing to it; I will heal my people and will let them enjoy abundant peace and security." (Jeremiah 33:6)

In The Morning

_____
_____
_____
_____
_____
_____
_____
_____
_____
_____

MARCH 2ND

"PLANTING WEEDS WON'T BLOOM FLOWERS

You planted weeds but wanted flowers. Now you're frustrated at what's blooming. Sound familiar?

See, God is not mocked; what one sows, they will reap. And if you're not happy about your harvest, why do you plant those seeds? (Galatians 6:7)

Remember, if you don't like what's growing, then you need to change your seed.

"The point is this: whoever sows sparingly will also reap sparingly, and whoever sows bountifully will also reap bountifully." (2 Corinthians 9:6)

In The Morning

_____

_____

_____

_____

_____

_____

_____

_____

_____

_____

_____

_____

MARCH 3ᴿᴰ

"KNOW WHEN TO GET UP"

Should I stay or should I go? That's a question that many ask of themselves.

See, it can be difficult rescuing yourself from a person, place, or relationship that means you no good.

But when you have that gut feeling, it's a sign that you need to go. (John 16:13) (Hebrews 3:7-8)

Remember, you have to learn to stop sitting at tables you no longer belong at.

It's time to get up!!!!

"Leave the presence of a fool, for there you do not meet words of knowledge." (Proverbs 14:7)

In The Morning

_____
_____
_____
_____
_____
_____
_____
_____
_____
_____

MARCH 4TH

"PRETTY WORDS"

Have you ever tried to describe the truth by using pretty words? See, pretty words are just that, pretty. It's pleasing and attractive to those that hear. But just because you say them, doesn't make it true.

Remember, pretty words are not necessarily true, and true words aren't always pretty.

"Little children, let us not love in words or talk but in deed and in truth." (1 John 3:18)

In The Morning

MARCH 5TH

"BE TEACHABLE"

Everybody knows them: People who know everything. At least, that's what they believe.

See, it's a dangerous thing to be a know-it-all. Because it means you're not teachable, and to be teachable means you have the mindset of a lifelong learner, and you're open to learning. (Hosea 4:6)

Truth is teachable; it is a foundation to spiritual growth, character development, and your walk with the Lord. (Proverbs 8:32-36)

Remember, no matter how anointed you THINK you are, you must be teachable - there is always something to learn.

"Although they claimed to be wise, they became fools," (Romans 1:22)

In The Morning

_____
_____
_____
_____
_____
_____
_____
_____
_____

MARCH 6TH

"A RECIPE FOR UNHAPPINESS"

There is one life that you can control, YOURS. So the question you have to ask yourself, *why am I comparing myself to someone else?*

See, comparison is a dangerous thing. It drains you of precious energy and leads to resentment. To sum it up, it's a recipe for unhappiness.

Remember, think of yourself as the Sun and others as the Moon. There is no comparison, both shine when it's their time!

"For we dare not make ourselves of the number or compare ourselves with some that commend themselves: but they who are measuring themselves by themselves, and comparing themselves among themselves, are not wise." (2 Corinthians 10:12)

IN THE MORNING

MARCH 7TH
"YOU'RE NOT BEING PUNISHED"

Have you ever been waiting for your blessing, yet nothing happens?

See, waiting on God can be one of the most challenging things you do. It's not about sitting around and watching the clock turn. NO!

It's an open invitation for you to believe in His wisdom and trust His plans, despite what you see. (2 Corinthians 5:7)

Remember, waiting isn't your punishment; it's your PREPARATION!!!

"Dear brothers and sisters, be patient as you wait for the Lord's return. Consider the farmers who patiently wait for the rains in the fall and in the spring. They eagerly look for the valuable harvest to ripen. You, too, must be patient. Take courage, for the coming of the Lord is near."(James 5:7-8)

IN THE MORNING

MARCH 8TH

"WHY WON'T YOU DO SOMETHING"

Have you ever thought, *why won't someone do something?* Yet, no one intervenes.

See, you can't bully others into stepping in. So instead of wanting someone else to do what you want, why don't you?

Remember, stop saying somebody should do something. YOU are the somebody.

"Mankind, he has told each of you what is good and what it is the LORD requires of you: to act justly, to love faithfulness, and to walk humbly with your God." (Micah 6:8)

In The Morning

_____
_____
_____
_____
_____
_____
_____
_____
_____
_____
_____
_____
_____
_____

MARCH 9TH

"A NECESSARY WRECK"

Often anxiety can rush into your life, making you think: I have to be, do or have something by a particular time frame. And when things don't go accordingly to plan, worry sits in. Sound familiar?

See, your time might not match God's time. And when you try to rush what He doesn't want right now, your plans will be demolished.

Remember, God will interrupt and wreck to bless you, for His will is going to be done, and His plan will prevail.

"Many are the plans in a person's heart, but it is the LORD's purpose that prevails." (Proverbs 19:21)

In The Morning

_____
_____
_____
_____
_____
_____
_____
_____
_____
_____
_____
_____

MARCH 10TH

"DISGUISED AS WHAT YOU WANT"

It would be easy if Satan came as he is often portrayed, with horns and a pitchfork, looking evil. No doubt everyone would flee. But what happens when he comes as something you want?

The truth is Satan disguises himself as an angel of light. This is why you have to be on guard and stand firm against all strategies and schemes he brings. (2 Corinthians 11:14) (Ephesians 6:11)

Remember, attacks from the enemy won't always feel like pain. Sometimes it feels like pleasure.

"For this reason, take up the whole armor of God so that you may be able to take a stand whenever evil comes. And when you have done everything you could, you will be able to stand firm." (Ephesians 6:13)

IN THE MORNING

_____
_____
_____
_____
_____
_____
_____
_____
_____
_____
_____

MARCH 11TH

"A LIE IS NOTHING WITHOUT POWER"

Lies, half-truths, and cover-ups are all nothing without the power you give it. The question is, are you giving any of them power?

See, everyone has been affected one way or the other by lies. And when you can no longer tell the truth because the lie sounds better, you've become dysfunctional.

Remember, for a lie to have power, it must be believed.

It's time to STOP believing the enemy and believe ONLY the Word of God. It will NEVER lie! (Numbers 23:19)

"God cannot tell lies! And so His promises and vows are two things that can never be changed. We have run to God for safety. Now His promises should greatly encourage us to take hold of the hope that is right in front of us." (Hebrews 6:18)

In The Morning

_____

_____

_____

_____

_____

_____

_____

_____

MARCH 12TH

"NOT EVERYONE'S CHOICE"

Rejection is one of the most common emotional wounds you will face in your daily life. Whether it's something small or big, it still hurts. The question is, how long do you let it bother you?

The truth is everyone has their own needs, and it's their legal right to want what they want. And once you understand the rejection isn't your reflection, you win.

Remember, you won't be everyone's choice - and that's okay. The opinions of others do NOT dictate your value as a person.

"As you come to Him, the living stone, rejected by men but chosen and precious in God's sight," (1 Peter 2:4)

In The Morning

_____
_____
_____
_____
_____
_____
_____
_____
_____
_____
_____
_____

MARCH 13TH

"YOU CAN'T CHANGE THEM"

How many times have you said, "If only they would..."?

See, we all have had someone that drives us crazy because we want better for them. But first and foremost, you take care of yourself.

Now that doesn't mean you don't care, or you love them less. But you can't trick or manipulate to make others do something that they're not ready for.

Remember, you will never change someone who doesn't see anything wrong with their actions or behavior. But YOU CAN change how you react to them.

"Accept other believers who are weak in faith, and don't argue with them about what they think is right or wrong." (Romans 14:1)

In The Morning

_____

_____

_____

_____

_____

_____

_____

_____

_____

MARCH 14TH

"SUFFERING IN SILENCE"

There are too many folks in this world that are suffering in silence. Most of the time, they are the strongest ones you don't even suspect: neighbors, colleagues, family, or church members. The question is, are you the one suffering?

See, even the "strong one" needs help too. And you can try to hide the pain; but hiding it won't make it go away.

Remember, someone right now is hurting, and you'll never know because they're suffering in silence.

"Come to me, all you who are weary and burdened, and I will give you rest. Take my yoke upon you and learn from me, for I am gentle and humble in heart, and you will find rest for your souls. For my yoke is easy and my burden is light." (Matthew 11:28-30)

In The Morning

_____

_____

_____

_____

_____

_____

_____

_____

_____

_____

_____

MARCH 15TH

"CHAOS ADDICTION OR PEACE"

When you're always living in a state of turmoil or drama, it's called "Chaos Addiction". The question is, does that describe YOU?

See, folks often get used to dysfunction. So when "peace of mind" comes -- what should be normal will appear as abnormal.

Remember, don't let "chaos addiction" have you questioning the peace of mind God is giving you.

"Peace I leave with you; my peace I give to you. Not as the world gives do I give to you. Let not your hearts be troubled, neither let them be afraid." (John 14:27)

In The Morning

_____
_____
_____
_____
_____
_____
_____
_____
_____
_____
_____
_____

MARCH 16TH

"A DIVINE APPOINTMENT"

Have you ever had high expectations that something would be in your favor, but just like that, things didn't work out. And now you're finding it difficult to deal with the unfulfilled promise.

Sound familiar?

Feeling disappointed, of course, doesn't feel great. And just because you want something doesn't mean that God wants it for you.

See, God knows the end and the beginning. And what you think is a disappointment is Him looking out for you. (Isaiah 46:10)

Remember, God will take your greatest disappointment, and reshape it to a divine appointment.

"The LORD Almighty has sworn, "Surely, as I have planned, so it will be, and as I have purposed, so it will happen." (Isaiah 14:24)

In The Morning

_____
_____
_____
_____
_____
_____
_____
_____

MARCH 17ᵀᴴ

"GOD HAS SOMETHING BETTER FOR ME"

Do you ever ask yourself the question, "Why is this happening to me?" Most of us do, especially when we lose or have been robbed of things we desperately wanted.

See, when losses occur, it takes tremendous faith to say, "God has something better for me." Yes, things can be harrowing and challenging, but God will never leave you empty. He will replace everything you lost. If He asks you to put something down, it's because He wants you to pick up something Greater! (Hebrews 11:40)

Remember, just because God didn't answer your prayers doesn't mean He's not listening. He has something better in store for you, and you don't have to chase what it is!

"Now to Him who is able to do exceedingly abundantly above all that we ask or think, according to the power that works in us," (Ephesians 3:20)

In The Morning

_____

_____

_____

_____

_____

_____

_____

MARCH 18TH

"A REPEATED CYCLE"

Have you ever found yourself going through the same repeated lesson over and over?

See, the lesson you couldn't learn the first time will come again through a different form. And until you conquer it, you will be trapped in a repeated cycle.

Remember, God will show you to teach you, and if you still can't get what He is trying to reveal, He will display it again and again!

"Let the wise hear and increase in learning, and the one who understands obtain guidance," (Proverbs 1:5)

IN THE MORNING

MARCH 19ᵀᴴ

"I'M NOT READY FOR THIS"

Ready or not, trouble is going to come. The question is, What do you do when it shows up?

See, it's not a question of if, but when--at some point, everyone faces difficulties. But it's how you handle them that makes the difference.

Remember, you might not have been ready for what comes, but you are built to go through it.

"Beloved, do not be surprised at the fiery trial that has come upon you, as though something strange were happening to you. But rejoice that you share in the sufferings of Christ, so that you may be overjoyed at the revelation of His glory." (1 Peter 4:12-13)

In The Morning

MARCH 20TH

"THE REVENGE ISN'T WORTH IT"

The first thing that many think about after being wronged or disrespected is, How can I get even?

Ralph Waldo Emerson says it best, "For every minute you are angry, you lose sixty seconds of happiness."

See, it seems easy to retaliate and strike back after someone has hurt you. But that doesn't mean that's what you should do.

The truth is - what YOU can do is one thing – and what God WILL DO is totally different. (Deuteronomy 32:35)

Remember, the best revenge is to remain silent and press on. Let your happiness speak volumes!

"May the LORD judge between you and me. And may the LORD avenge the wrongs you have done to me, but my hand will not touch you." (1 Samuel 24:12)

In The Morning

_____
_____
_____
_____
_____
_____
_____
_____
_____

MARCH 21ST

"BUT IS IT HEALTHY?"

It's a delicious hot fudge ice cream sundae topped with whipped cream and nuts. And you have to take a bite, but you forgot you're allergic to nuts.

See, that's how life can be. Some things look good to the eye, but deep inside, they can kill you.

Remember, you might want what you want, but it doesn't mean it's healthy for you!!!

"You say, "I am allowed to do anything"—but not everything is good for you. And even though "I am allowed to do anything," I must not become a slave to anything." (1 Corinthians 6:12)

In The Morning

MARCH 22ND

"IT'S OVERDUE"

Most of us don't like waiting. We become irritated waiting in long lines, frustrated with long red lights, and annoyed when food takes too long. The question is: Do you act the same while waiting on God?

See, waiting on the Lord can be difficult. It's not like the wait that you do at the doctor's office, where you dread it. When you wait on the Lord, it's going to require an act of faith. (Psalm 27:13-14)

Remember, it might feel like it's overdue, but God will act when it's your time.

For now - be patient!

"But they who wait for the Lord shall renew their strength; they shall mount up with wings like eagles; they shall run and not be weary; they shall walk and not faint." (Isaiah 40:31)

In The Morning

_____
_____
_____
_____
_____
_____
_____
_____

MARCH 23ʳᴰ

"(THIS) THAT I'M GOING THROUGH"

Everyone has problems. Even those that pretend to have a "perfect life" are still dealing with issues.

See, your troubles and trials aren't mute or blind to God. He knows all about them. (Psalm 139:16)

Remember, it doesn't matter what your (this) is -God is with you.

"God is our refuge and strength, A very present help in trouble." (Psalm 46:1)

In The Morning

MARCH 24TH

"THE BANANA PEELS ON THE GROUND"

Slipping on a banana peel might be funny to those who see it, but it could be dangerous to the one that slips and falls.

But that's how the enemy tries to come for you. He thinks he's funny and conniving, trying to get you to fall.

But the jokes on him – because you're grounded with the Word of God. (Colossians 2:7)

Remember, make sure you watch where you step, don't get tricked by the banana peels the enemy throws on the ground.

"Your word is a lamp to my feet and a light to my path." (Psalm 119:105)

In The Morning

_____
_____
_____
_____
_____
_____
_____
_____
_____
_____
_____
_____
_____

MARCH 25TH

"GOD TOLD ME TO TELL YOU..."

Often people can come to you claiming that God told them to tell you something. The question is: Do you take heed to it?

See, God can use others for confirmation and revelation, but you must learn to use discernment. Because what God won't do -- is use someone to tell you something that contradicts His will for you. (1 Kings 13:16-19)

Remember, there are a lot of false prophets running around, don't get fooled by one. (1 John 4:1)

"For false Messiahs and false prophets will appear; they will perform great miracles and wonders in order to deceive even God's chosen people, if possible." (Matthew 24:24)

In The Morning

_____
_____
_____
_____
_____
_____
_____
_____
_____
_____
_____
_____

MARCH 26TH

"BUT I TOLD YOU MY PAIN"

"Why did I have to open my mouth?!" That's a question that many ask after they confided in who they THOUGHT was a confidant —only to be betrayed.

See, sometimes folks want a listening ear. So they openly share their suffering, but at what cost?

Remember, some of the worst pain you will experience is getting hurt by the person you told your pain to.

So if you want someone to talk to – Go to God; He's ready and waiting to hear!

"The eyes of the LORD are on the righteous, and His ears are inclined to their cry." (Psalm 34:15)

In The Morning

MARCH 27TH

"THE FIGHT OF MY LIFE"

They are just sitting around wondering how it's going to end. Sound familiar?

See, when it comes down to it, most of our fear comes from the unknown. So it's just easy to go to the worst-case scenario.

But you have hope - God knows how this is going to end. And you're destined to WIN!!! (Jeremiah 29:11)

Remember, you might be in the fight of your life, but it's a fixed fight.

YOU WIN!!!!

"But thanks be to God, who in Christ always leads us in triumphal procession, and through us spreads the fragrance of the knowledge of him everywhere." (2 Corinthians 2:14)

In The Morning

_____

_____

_____

_____

_____

_____

_____

_____

_____

MARCH 28TH

"BURYING THE PAIN"

Some folks go over, under, and around their problems. Others shop, eat and try to medicate the pain away. The question is: Which do you do?

See, it doesn't matter how you try to avoid your situation; because it will never go away until you face it.

Remember, you can't bury the pain away; you have to go THROUGH it!

"So do not fear, for I am with you; do not be dismayed, for I am your God. I will strengthen you and help you; I will uphold you with my righteous right hand." (Isaiah 41:10)

In The Morning

MARCH 29TH

"THE MESSAGE"

How many times have you checked your phone while waiting for someone to respond?

What about the times you looked a person in the eye and waited for them to speak - only to realize they were purposely mute?

See, no matter what the delay is, anxiety will start to sit in while you wait. But a lack of response is a powerful one.

Remember, getting "no message" IS YOUR MESSAGE.

"For he has not arranged his words against me, Nor will I reply to him with your arguments. (Job 32:14)

IN THE MORNING

_____
_____
_____
_____
_____
_____
_____
_____
_____
_____
_____
_____
_____

MARCH 30TH

"WHERE'S THE FOCUS"

Have you ever been so focused on the problems that you forget about God's promises for your life?

See, it's easy to focus on the trouble, burdens, and heartache that's taken place. But when you do that, your target becomes on your predicament and NOT God.

In times of trials, there should be one focus - GOD. Let your mind be centered on His character and faithfulness.

Remember, His power is your focus, not your problems.

"You will keep in perfect peace all who trust in you, all whose thoughts are fixed on you!" (Isaiah 26:3)

In The Morning

MARCH 31ST

"BAND-AIDS WON'T FIX IT"

You got cut! And you desperately want it to heal. So you stick a Band-Aid on it. But underneath - there is an infection brewing.

See, pain is inevitable. And although the wound may not be your fault, the healing is your responsibility.

Remember, all wounds in life won't heal with Band-Aids alone – some are going to require serious treatment to be healed.

"Behold, I will bring to it health and healing, and I will heal them and reveal to them abundance of prosperity and security." (Jeremiah 33:6)

IN THE MORNING

APRIL 1ˢᵀ

"IT'S YOUR RESPONSE THAT COUNTS"

You've been talked about, dragged in the mud, and now you want to address your foes. Sound familiar?

See, it's natural to want to defend yourself. But one of the most powerful things you can say to someone - isn't a word. It's NOTHING.

Remember, people are going to be people. But it's your responsibility in how you deal with them that matters.

Before you respond: PRAY and THINK!

"Understand this, my dear brothers and sisters: You must all be quick to listen, slow to speak, and slow to get angry." (James 1:19)

In The Morning

_____
_____
_____
_____
_____
_____
_____
_____
_____
_____
_____
_____

APRIL 2ND

"PROTECT YOUR PEACE, PERIOD"

There comes a time in everyone's life where you have to decide to protect your peace. The question is: Are you protecting it?

See, a big part of self-care and self-love is ensuring that your peace is protected by all means necessary.

So even if others get upset by your decision. You protect YOU.

Remember, protect your peace, PERIOD!

"Peace I leave with you; my peace I give to you. Not as the world gives do I give to you. Let not your hearts be troubled, neither let them be afraid." (John 14:27)

In The Morning

_____
_____
_____
_____
_____
_____
_____
_____
_____
_____
_____
_____
_____

APRIL 3ᴿᴰ

"TAKE A LOOK IN THE MIRROR"

"Fix the lighting, get the backdrop right, and find the right pose and facial expression." I've just described the perfect picture in front of the camera, known as a - SELFIE.

See, when you take a selfie, you try to make sure it portrays you in a positive and best light. No one will ever display a lousy picture.

But what happens when the lines get blurred, and you can't tell the difference between self and your altered image?

Remember, don't be the person who stands in front of the camera instead of the mirror. Pictures can be manipulated, but the mirror will expose your truth.

It's time to look in the mirror!!!

"And no creature is hidden from his sight, but all are naked and exposed to the eyes of him to whom we must give account." (Hebrews 4:13)

In The Morning

_____
_____
_____
_____
_____
_____
_____
_____

APRIL 4TH

"PRISON OF PARADISE"

Prisons are buildings in which people are legally held as a punishment for a crime they have committed. But have you ever thought about the prisons that you put yourself in?

See, the lack of forgiveness is one of the biggest imprisonments in spiritual growth. And your memories in life store everything – the good, bad and ugly. But if you can't let go of the pain and hurt you've endured, you'll lock yourself up.

Remember, if you're not healed, you will view your prison as paradise.

"Heal me, O LORD, and I shall be healed; save me, and I shall be saved, for you are my praise." (Jeremiah 17:4)

IN THE MORNING

_____

_____

_____

_____

_____

_____

_____

_____

_____

_____

_____

APRIL 5TH

"WEAPONS OR MEDICINE"

Loving words can have just as big of an impact on a person as hateful ones do. The question is: How are you using the words that come out of your mouth?

See, life and death are in the power of the tongue. And it's up to YOU to determine if you're going to build up or tear down. (Proverbs 18:21)

Remember, be careful with your words – they can be weapons or medicine.

"He who guards his mouth and tongue keeps his soul from distress." (Proverbs 21:23)

IN THE MORNING

_____
_____
_____
_____
_____
_____
_____
_____
_____
_____
_____
_____

APRIL 6TH

"WE'RE ON DIFFERENT PAGES"

You strive for happiness and peace. But your circle lives in a life of stress, disorder, and drama. Sound familiar?

See, everyone isn't going to be on the same page as you. And that's okay - YOU just have to make sure you don't take on their chaos.

Remember, their version of happiness may be your version of frustration. Be careful not to covet the lives of others.

"Do not be unequally yoked with unbelievers. For what partnership has righteousness with lawlessness? Or what fellowship has light with darkness?" (2 Corinthians 6:14)

In The Morning

APRIL 7TH

"THEY WILL NEVER GIVE IT TO YOU"

It was their fault, and you apologized. But you're still waiting on an apology from them. Sound familiar?

See, it doesn't matter if the betrayal came from a romantic relationship, friendship, or family member. Blaming yourself for someone else's behavior isn't yours to own.

Remember, be okay with an apology you will never get. The truth is - some folks are too prideful to utter the words!

"So watch yourselves. "If your brother or sister sins against you, rebuke them; and if they repent, forgive them. Even if they sin against you seven times in a day and seven times come back to you saying, 'I repent,' you must forgive them." (Luke 17:3-4)

In The Morning

_____
_____
_____
_____
_____
_____
_____
_____
_____
_____
_____
_____
_____

APRIL 8TH

"MEAN WHAT YOU SAY & SAY WHAT YOU MEAN"

You have something to say, but you don't know how to say it. Yet - You think others know what you mean. Sound familiar?

See, it's not always easy to tell people how you feel – but it's necessary. And you can't get mad or irritated when they have no idea what you're thinking.

Remember, use your words; folks aren't mind readers!

"A word fitly spoken is like apples of gold in settings of silver." (Proverbs 25:11)

In The Morning

_____
_____
_____
_____
_____
_____
_____
_____
_____
_____
_____
_____
_____
_____
_____

APRIL 9TH

"IT'S JUST CHILDISH"

Silly, immature, and juvenile - that describes a childish person. The question is: Do you know any?

See, whether we want to admit it or not; everyone can be a little immature from time to time. But there's a vast difference between having an occasional moment of immaturity and being an immature person.

Remember, childish folks will do childish things. Just make sure you don't become childish by applauding the foolery.

"When I was a child, I spoke and thought and reasoned as a child. But when I grew up, I put away childish things." (1 Corinthians 13:11)

In The Morning

APRIL 10TH

"A VICTIM OF ABSENCE"

Some folks can drain the life and energy out of you. And if you're not careful - You will become a victim of their abuse.

See, when you're used to dysfunction, normal behavior seems abnormal. But there comes a time that you have to say, "I've had enough."

Remember, before you become a victim of anyone's abuse, let them become a victim of your absence.

"The prudent see danger and take cover, but the simple keep going and suffer the consequences." (Proverbs 22:3)

In The Morning

APRIL 11TH

"DID YOU LET IT GO OR BURY IT?"

Letting go is to stop holding on to something or someone. To bury is to cover- hide down completely. The question is: Which are you doing?

See, it's easy to say you've let go. But have you really if all you're doing is burying the pain?

Remember, often, what you think you're letting go of, is being buried. And what's planted will grow!!!

"Sow for yourselves righteousness; reap steadfast love; break up your fallow ground, for it is the time to seek the LORD, that He may come and rain righteousness upon you." (Hosea 10:12)

IN THE MORNING

_____

_____

_____

_____

_____

_____

_____

_____

_____

_____

_____

_____

APRIL 12TH

"LET IT RAIN"

Rain is nothing but water droplets from the clouds. And clouds can cause gloom, suspicion, trouble, or worry. The question is: Are you okay when the rain comes?

See, rain isn't a bad thing. Yes, you're going to become wet if you don't have coverage. But the rain causes your seed to grow.

What do I mean? The same folks that tried to destroy you and brought the storms in your life. Didn't realize you would blossom when the rain came.

"Shower, O heavens, from above, and let the clouds rain down righteousness; let the earth open, that salvation and righteousness may bear fruit; let the earth cause them both to sprout; I, the LORD have created it." (Isaiah 45:8)

IN THE MORNING

APRIL 13TH

"WHAT IS YOUR ATTITUDE SAYING?"

Energy is your mental activity. And attitude is your way of thinking or behavior. The question is: How are you coming off?

See, sometimes folks think because they don't say anything, it's okay. But they forget their attitude is speaking.

Remember, your energy will always introduce you before you open your mouth.

"Let the Spirit renew your thoughts and attitudes." (Ephesians 4:23)

IN THE MORNING

APRIL 14TH

"USE YOUR KEYS WISELY"

Keys are something that most people have. Whether it's to their homes, cars, or lockers, they're used to open and lock doors.

But the question is, are you using them wisely?

Remember, make sure you use your keys daily; open new possibilities, lockout problems, and grant access to what God has placed in you!

"Ask, and it will be given to you; seek, and you will find; knock, and it will be opened to you. For everyone who asks, receives; and the one who seeks, finds; and to the one who knocks, it will be opened." (Matthew 7:7-8)

In The Morning

APRIL 15TH

"WALKING AROUND WITH SCISSORS"

Scissors are used to cut paper, cloth, or other thin material. So if you see someone walking around with scissors, they're probably about to do some cutting.

The question is: What are you using your scissors for?

See, folks cut people out of their lives all the time. Sometimes it's intentional, and other times they don't even realize they're doing it.

Remember, be careful how you choose to leave people. You never know who God will have you back in front of them again.

"The LORD said to my Lord, "Sit in the place of honor at my right hand until I humble your enemies, making them a footstool under your feet." (Psalm 110:1)

In The Morning

_____
_____
_____
_____
_____
_____
_____
_____
_____
_____

APRIL 16TH

"THEY'VE MOVED ON"

When someone walks out of your life, it hurts. But it hurts more when you can't let go.

See, folks come in our lives for a reason and a season. Everyone isn't meant to stay. And when they decide to go - you have to let them.

Remember, they've moved on. Now it's time to release the anger so you can live!

"They went out from us, but they did not really belong to us. For if they had belonged to us, they would have remained with us; but their going showed that none of them belonged to us." (1 John 2:19)

In The Morning

_____
_____
_____
_____
_____
_____
_____
_____
_____
_____
_____

APRIL 17ᵀᴴ

"YOUR "YES" DOESN'T NEED COUNSEL"

God gave you a "YES," and you've accepted it. But folks are trying to tell you otherwise. Sound familiar?

See, folks always have something to say. So let them talk! Because what they say will never trump over God's Word.

Remember, God has given you favor for a "YES." No one can CANCEL or COUNSEL you out of His "YES"!

"God is not a man, that He should lie, or a son of man, that He should change His mind. Does He speak and not act? Does He promise and not fulfill?" (Numbers 23:19)

In The Morning

APRIL 18TH

"THE LETDOWN"

Have you ever been let down, hurt or disappointed? And because of the hurt, you didn't know what to do next. Sound familiar?

See, in life, disappointments are going to come. But it's how you deal with them that matters.

Remember, never allow your "letdown" to shut you down!!!!

"We are pressed on every side by troubles, but we are not crushed. We are perplexed, but not driven to despair. We are hunted down, but never abandoned by God. We get knocked down, but we are not destroyed." (2 Corinthians 4:8-9)

In The Morning

APRIL 19TH

"COMMITTED TO THE DEADLINE OR DELAY?"

Delays are a period in which something is late or postponed. Deadlines are the latest time or date in which something should be completed. The question is: Which has your focus?

Yes, you want it now. But what's the cost to you if you get it before you're ready?

Remember, commitment with a deadline is NOT faithfulness!!!!!

"For the revelation awaits an appointed time; it speaks of the end and will not prove false. Though it lingers, wait for it; it will certainly come and will not delay." (Habakkuk 2:3)

"But those who wait upon the LORD will renew their strength; they will mount up with wings like eagles; they will run and not grow weary; they will walk and not faint." (Isaiah 40:31)

In The Morning

APRIL 20TH

"SABOTAGING THE SHIP"

When folks want to destroy, damage, or obstruct something deliberately, they sabotage it. The question is: What are you sabotaging in your own life?

See, you may not be aware that you're doing something on purpose. But if you're continually pushing away who or what was sent to help you – that's sabotage.

Remember, STOP sabotaging the ship that was sent to rescue YOU! (Luke 5:3-10)

"Pride goes before destruction, and a haughty spirit before a fall." (Proverbs 16:18)

In The Morning

_____
_____
_____
_____
_____
_____
_____
_____
_____
_____
_____

APRIL 21ST

"A PROTECTED HEART"

You have given your heart to this one and that one. Yet, it's been broken repeatedly. Sound familiar?

See, no one wants a broken heart. And a person has every right to protect who they give their heart to.

So the best way to protect your heart - is to give it to God and let Him QUALIFY who deserves the space in it!

"Give me your heart, my son, And let your eyes delight in my ways." (Proverbs 23:26)

IN THE MORNING

APRIL 22ND

"THE STALKER"

God removed it. Yet you still can't let it go. Sound familiar? I get it. You wanted it and didn't want it to go or end. But it did. So now what?

Now you leave it alone!

Remember, when God blocks it, you don't need to stalk it!!!

"The LORD keeps you from all harm and watches over your life." (Psalm 121:7)

In The Morning

___
___
___
___
___
___
___
___
___
___
___
___
___
___
___
___
___
___

APRIL 23ᴿᴰ

"BUT YOU GOT WHAT YOU WANTED"

You wanted it badly. But when you finally got it. It wasn't what you expected. Sound familiar?

See, everything isn't as it seems. And what you "THOUGHT" was going to be a blessing. Can end up hurting and harming you.

Remember, everything isn't God-sent!

"Stay alert! Watch out for your great enemy, the devil. He prowls around like a roaring lion, looking for someone to devour." (1 Peter 5:8)

In The Morning

APRIL 24TH

"ARE YOU GOING TO BE IN FAITH OR IN YOUR FEELINGS?"

Faith is confidence in what we hope for and assurance about what we do not see. (Hebrews 11:1) Feelings are your emotional state. The question is: Which are you leading with?

See, folks can be cruel and mean - causing your feelings to hurt. But just because they threw the "stone" doesn't mean you have to react to it. (Proverbs 28:26)

Remember, you have to let your faith be more significant than your feelings.

"For God gave us a spirit not of fear but of power and love and self-control." (2 Timothy 1:7)

In The Morning

___
___
___
___
___
___
___
___
___
___

APRIL 25TH

"THEIR OPINION BUT YOUR ASSIGNMENT"

You had the vision and ran with it. But someone had something to say about it. So you stopped. Sound familiar?

See, folks are always going to have something to say. If you didn't do it, they would claim, "You're lazy." And if you did do it, "You're doing too much."

So, do YOU!

Remember, don't let the opinions of others STOP the assignment God has called you for.

"For this reason I remind you to fan into flame the gift of God, which is in you through the laying on of my hands." (2 Timothy 1:6)

In The Morning

_____
_____
_____
_____
_____
_____
_____
_____
_____
_____
_____
_____

APRIL 26TH

"OUT OF VIP"

When a person is in the VIP section, they're entitled to many perks—making it the place to be. But then you have the balcony section, which is in the back. And it's the worst spot to be.

The question is: Where are you allowing folks in your life?

See, I'm sure you think you don't have a stage or auditorium. So this doesn't apply to you. But it does if you keep allowing folks to be in your life that shouldn't be.

Remember, there are times that you need to up and move some people from the VIP section of your life and sit them in a regular balcony seat!

"No one can serve two masters; for either he will hate the one and love the other, or he will be devoted to the one and despise the other. You cannot serve God and mammon [money, possessions, fame, status, or whatever is valued more than the Lord]." (Matthew 6:24)(AMP)

In The Morning

_____
_____
_____
_____
_____
_____
_____
_____

APRIL 27ᵀᴴ

"THE OBSESSION"

When a person is obsessed, they're preoccupied with the state of being with someone or something. The question is: Are you obsessed?

See, it's a knee-jerk reaction to say no. But if you can't stop watching and lurking into what others are doing - you're obsessed!

Remember, you will never find out the life you should have if you become obsessed with everyone else's.

BE YOU!!!!!!!!

"Do not love the world or the things in the world. If anyone loves the world, the love of the Father is not in him. For all that is in the world—the desires of the flesh and the desires of the eyes and pride in possessions—is not from the Father, but is from the world. And the world is passing away along with its desires, but whoever does the will of God abides forever." (1 John 2:15-17)

In The Morning

_____
_____
_____
_____
_____
_____
_____
_____

APRIL 28TH

"LET THEM BE MAD"

Have you ever come across someone that didn't like you? And you had no reason at all why they felt the way they did.

See, some folk's attitude and hatred towards you have nothing to do with you. It's all about them.

So don't apologize for the favor over your life. Let them be mad.

"For you bless the righteous, O LORD; you cover him with favor as with a shield." (Psalm 5:12)

In The Morning

APRIL 29ᵀᴴ

"FIGHT FOR IT"

Marriage. Job. Family. Relationships. From every which way you turn, you're catching hell. And because of it, you're ready to give up. Sound familiar?

See, there are some things in life that you must walk away from. Then there are things that you have to fight for.

Remember, everything isn't toxic. That's why you must lean on the Lord and listen for discernment. It could be you're under attack!!!! (1 Kings 3:9)

"For we do not wrestle against flesh and blood, but against the rulers, against the authorities, against the cosmic powers over this present darkness, against the spiritual forces of evil in the heavenly places." (Ephesians 6:12)

IN THE MORNING

_____
_____
_____
_____
_____
_____
_____
_____
_____
_____
_____
_____

APRIL 30TH

"THE EAR THAT LISTENS"

Have you ever gone through a difficult time and just wanted someone there to listen to you? And you confide in them, but then they become your Public Relations Manager getting your story out.

See, it's a knee-jerk reaction to vent to someone that should be a trusted confidant about struggles that you're enduring. But should they be trusted?

Remember, some folks are excellent listeners. (Gossipers) And just because they're listening doesn't mean that they have a concerned heart or a quiet mouth!

"Whoever slanders his neighbor secretly I will destroy. Whoever has a haughty look and an arrogant heart I will not endure." (Psalm 101:5)

In The Morning

MAY 1ST

"THE KNOW-IT-ALL"

They came into your life to help you. But because you know-it-all, you're not trying to receive anything they say. Sound familiar?

See, it's a dangerous thing for a person to know EVERYTHING and can't be taught. The teacher will rise when the student is ready. The question is: Are you ready?

Remember, don't let you and your attitude hate on the person that God sent to bless you. Learn to close your mouth before your door gets closed!!!!

"Arrogant know-it-alls stir up discord, but wise men and women listen to each other's counsel." (Proverbs 13:10)

In The Morning

MAY 2ND

"JUST SAY NO!"

They call, and you take off running. Sound familiar?

See, some folks in this world can drain you dry. But that's not on them. It's on YOU for allowing them to.

Remember, there comes a time that you have to stop saying YES to everything and say NO!!!!!

"You say, "I am allowed to do anything"—but not everything is good for you. And even though "I am allowed to do anything," I must not become a slave to anything." (1 Corinthians 6:12)

In The Morning

MAY 3RD

"THE ANOINTED"

The anointing is what empowers a man or a woman to function in their supernatural authority. The question is: Are you anointed?

See the oil costs. And some folks think because you're anointed, you're exempt from trials and tribulations. WRONG!

Remember, the fact that "they" don't like you won't make you unanointed.

"Do not touch my anointed ones; do my prophets no harm." (Psalm 105:15)

In The Morning

_____
_____
_____
_____
_____
_____
_____
_____
_____
_____
_____
_____
_____
_____
_____

MAY 4ᵀᴴ

"TAKE THE MEDICINE PLEASE"

When someone is sick, it's usually medicine that would be the cure to heal them. But what happens when they refuse to take the meds?

The truth is you can't force someone to be healed. They have to want it for themselves.

Remember, you can't keep bringing medicine to folks who love being sick!

"And if anyone will not receive you or listen to your words, shake off the dust from your feet when you leave that house or town." (Matthew 10:14)

In The Morning

_____
_____
_____
_____
_____
_____
_____
_____
_____
_____

MAY 5TH

"I NEED TO LOSE WEIGHT"

When you hear someone say they need to lose weight. It is usually the weight on their body. But have you ever thought about the weight that isn't seen?

See, there are a lot of folks that need to lose weight. But it's not the kind you think.

Remember, the weight you need to lose isn't on your body. Start shedding the pounds of self-sabotage, grudges, obligations, guilt, blame, and regret.

Lose them TODAY!!!!

"And in that day his burden will depart from your shoulder, and his yoke from your neck; and the yoke will be broken because of the fat." (Isaiah 10:27)

In The Morning

_____
_____
_____
_____
_____
_____
_____
_____
_____

MAY 6™

"THE HAUNTING"

Have you ever been hurt so bad that it was hard to get over it? And the person that hurt you went on as if nothing happened.

See, it's hurtful when you see the one that caused the pain, live happily ever after. But that doesn't mean that you have to keep reliving your hurt over and over.

Remember, you're responsible for how long you let what hurt you, HAUNT you!!!

"Be strong and courageous. Do not fear or be in dread of them, for it is the Lord your God who goes with you. He will not leave you or forsake you." (Deuteronomy 31:6)

IN THE MORNING

MAY 7TH
"IT'S NO FUN WHEN THE RABBIT HAS THE GUN"

Have you ever been quick to talk about what other people are going through? But then, when you hear that someone said something about you, you're ready to set it off.

See, it's no fun when the rabbit has the gun. So instead of talking about them, pray for them. The truth is you don't know what storm God has called them to go through!!!

Remember, STOP letting your tongue mention others' faults. YOU have faults too, and they also have tongues!

"For in the same way you judge others, you will be judged, and with the measure you use, it will be measured to you." (Matthew 7:2)

In The Morning

MAY 8TH

"KNIFE WOUNDS"

Have you ever hurt someone, then got upset because they were struggling to get over it?

See, once you stab someone. You don't get to have a preference on the healing from your knife wound.

Remember, STOP wounding folks and expecting them to heal on your terms!

"For the wrongdoer will be paid back for the wrong he has done, and there is no partiality." (Colossians 3:25)

In The Morning

MAY 9TH

"THE CLOSURE"

Closure is the act or process of closing something. The question is: What are you still needing closure on?

See, sometimes you have to learn to accept an apology that you will never get.

YES! They might have hurt you and ran your name in the mud. But it doesn't mean you get to do tit for tat. (Romans 12:19)

Remember, instead of clapping back, the closure you need is to close your mouth and move on!!!!!

"The LORD will fight for you while you keep silent." (Exodus 14:14)

IN THE MORNING

MAY 10TH

"WHO DO I RUN TOO?"

No one will ever be exempt from tribulations in this life. Whether big or small, we all will encounter them.

However, when they do come, who do you run to?

See, it's easy to run to the phone and tell your troubles to a friend or relative. But what they can do is one thing and what the Lord WILL do is another. (1 Peter 5:7)

Remember, you can't keep running to man for your answers. Instead, choose to run to the Lord and His throne before you pick up the telephone.

"I run to you, God; I run for dear life." (Psalm 31:1) MSG

In The Morning

_____
_____
_____
_____
_____
_____
_____
_____
_____
_____
_____
_____

MAY 11TH

"I'M OFFENDED"

When someone is offended, it's a result of a perceived insult. The question is: Who's offended you?

See, some folks will always throw rocks at you. And some are even going to hide their hands. But it's what you do after the "rock" has been thrown that matters.

Remember, for you to be insulted, you must first learn to value their opinion. And being offended is YOUR choice!!!!!

"Do not pay attention to every word that is spoken," (Ecclesiastes 7:21)

IN THE MORNING

MAY 12TH

"THE MONUMENT"

Monuments are typically structures or sites that are of historical importance and interest. The question is: When are you going to tear down your monument?

See, I'm sure you think that you don't have one. But you do if you keep idolizing and revisiting a particular season in your life.

Remember, seasons come and go. So STOP letting what was for a moment be a monument in your life!!!!!

"For everything there is a season, a time for every activity under heaven." (Ecclesiastes 3:1)

In The Morning

_____
_____
_____
_____
_____
_____
_____
_____
_____
_____
_____
_____

MAY 13TH

"THE SUBSTITUTE"

Substitutes are used to serve in place of people or things. The question is: What substitutes are you allowing?

See, just because it's gone doesn't mean you need to rush to replace it.

STOP accepting what God didn't send. Be patient enough to wait on His REAL THING!!!!!!!!

"Wait for the Lord; be strong, and let your heart take courage; wait for the Lord!" (Psalm 27:14)

In The Morning

_____

_____

_____

_____

_____

_____

_____

_____

_____

_____

_____

_____

_____

_____

MAY 14TH

"DO YOU WANT TO LEARN OR BE JEALOUS?"

Have you ever seen someone doing exactly what you wanted to do? Rather than ask them about it, you decided to talk about them instead.

See, that's called jealousy. And it's a dangerous thing to be jealous of someone due to their achievements. (Job 5:2)

Remember, STOP gossiping about the person you should be learning from!

"An intelligent heart acquires knowledge, and the ear of the wise seeks knowledge." (Proverbs 18:15)

In The Morning

_____
_____
_____
_____
_____
_____
_____
_____
_____
_____
_____
_____

MAY 15TH

"TEACH ME HOW TO SWIM"

Swimming is a fun sport. It allows one to propel themselves through water using their arms and legs. However, everyone doesn't like to swim, usually because they don't know-how.

The question is: Who would you take swimming lessons from?

See, if you don't know how to swim, you should get expertise from someone who knows how. But that's not always the case.

Remember, you will never learn how to swim if you keep taking lessons from drowning people!!!!!!!!!!

"Whoever walks with the wise becomes wise, but the companion of fools will suffer harm." (Proverbs 13:20)

In The Morning

MAY 16ᵀᴴ

"THIS ISN'T MY PLAN"

There are times when things don't go as planned. Whether the job you wanted fell through, the relationship ended unexpectedly, or a beautiful bundle of joy arrived that you didn't think was possible.

See, life will repeatedly remind us that God is in control. In other words, we can make all the plans that we want. But it's the Lord's plan that WILL prevail. (Proverbs 19:21)

Remember, God may change your plans, but His plans and purposes are always greater than what you planned.

"For I know the plans I have for you," declares the LORD, "plans to prosper you and not to harm you, plans to give you hope and a future." (Jeremiah 29:11)

In The Morning

_____
_____
_____
_____
_____
_____
_____
_____
_____
_____

MAY 17ᵀᴴ

"BLEEDING ON THE WIRE"

It's something that you wanted. But the time is up. And you can't seem to let go.

See, there is a season and a time for everything in your life. And when "they" decide to go - no matter how bad it hurts. You have to let them. (Ecclesiastes 3:1)

Remember, if you choose to keep hanging on to someone. You'll find yourself bleeding on the "wire" you can't let go of.

"The righteous keep moving forward, and those with clean hands become stronger and stronger." (Job 17:9)

In The Morning

MAY 18TH

"ARE YOU IN A CIRCLE OR A CAGE?"

You hang around them, but they bring you down. Sound familiar? See, there comes a time that you have to evaluate your circle.

And just because you started with them. That doesn't mean you need to end with them.

Remember, if you look around your circle and the folks in it aren't inspiring you. Well, you don't have a circle; you have a cage!

"Do not be deceived: "Bad company corrupts good character." (1 Corinthians 15:33)

IN THE MORNING

MAY 19TH

"NO UGLY WORDS"

They hurt you, and now you want to hurt them. Sound familiar? See, sometimes you have to be just done. YES! What they did was wrong. But it's not for you to repay. (Deuteronomy 32:35)

Remember, you don't need any ugly words. No goodbyes. YOU just need to be DONE!!!!

"Beloved, never avenge yourselves, but leave it to the wrath of God, for it is written, "Vengeance is mine, I will repay, says the Lord." (Romans 12:19)

In The Morning

_____
_____
_____
_____
_____
_____
_____
_____
_____
_____
_____
_____
_____
_____
_____
_____

MAY 20TH

"GOD'S REPUTATION"

Worried, frustrated, and not sure what to do. Is that your situation?

See, the same God that rescued you before. Is the same God that's watching over you NOW!

Remember, God isn't going to wreck His reputation on you. IT IS WELL!!!!

"God is not a man, so he does not lie. He is not human, so He does not change his mind. Has He ever spoken and failed to act? Has He ever promised and not carried it through?" (Numbers 23:19)

In The Morning

_____
_____
_____
_____
_____
_____
_____
_____
_____
_____
_____
_____
_____
_____
_____

MAY 21ST

"THE BITTER HEART"

Have you ever tasted something bitter? Now imagine taking that taste and turning it into an emotion of resentfulness.

See, when you've been done wrong, it can cause your heart to become bitter. Making you want to pop and set it off. But you can't do that.

Remember, you can't trust your tongue when your heart becomes bitter. Just hush until you HEAL!!!!

"See to it that no one fails to obtain the grace of God; that no "root of bitterness" springs up and causes trouble, and by it many become defiled;" (Hebrews 12:15)

In The Morning

MAY 22ND

"THE UPDATE"

You've tried to move on. But folks keep telling you updates about them. Sound familiar?

See, there comes a time that you have to release everything. And that means you go on about your business without follow-ups.

What do I mean? STOP letting folks update you on people, places, and things that no longer concern you!

"Make it your goal to live a quiet life, minding your own business and working with your hands, just as we instructed you before." (1 Thessalonians 4:11)

In The Morning

MAY 23ᴿᴰ

"HE SAYS, SHE SAYS, THEY SAY"

Have you ever been upset because of what "they" said about you? See, folks have a way of talking. But it's up to you if you choose to listen.

Remember, if you keep listening to what everyone says, you will never hear what God is saying!

"So pay attention to how you hear. To those who listen to my teaching, more understanding will be given. But for those who are not listening, even what they think they understand will be taken away from them." (Luke 8:18)

In The Morning

_____
_____
_____
_____
_____
_____
_____
_____
_____
_____
_____
_____
_____
_____
_____

MAY 24TH

"LOVE FROM THE BALCONY"

They've hurt you to the core. And now they want forgiveness. Sound familiar?

See, sometimes you have to learn to love folks from afar. Now, does that mean you're still mad? NO!

But it does mean you're choosing to forgive and move on instead.

Remember, some people don't deserve you back. Start loving them from the balcony seat!

"So watch yourselves. "If your brother or sister sins against you, rebuke them; and if they repent, forgive them. Even if they sin against you seven times in a day and seven times come back to you saying, 'I repent,' you must forgive them."" (Luke 17:3-4)

In The Morning

MAY 25TH

"WRAPPED IN GOODBYE"

It's done and over with it. But it's hard for you to let it go. Sound familiar?

See, it doesn't matter what "it" is. Goodbyes can be challenging, but sometimes they're necessary.

Remember, your greatest and biggest blessing will come wrapped in the word, GOODBYE!

"For I know the plans I have for you," declares the LORD, "plans to prosper you and not to harm you, plans to give you hope and a future." (Jeremiah 29:11)

In The Morning

MAY 26TH

"THE BULLDOZERS"

It's the empire that you have built and always wanted. But it keeps falling apart. Sound familiar?

See, with success will come haters. And often, it's the ones that are closest to you – putting the cracks in your foundation.

Remember, you can't build your empire with "bulldozers" surrounding you.

"Everyone then who hears these words of mine and does them will be like a wise man who built his house on the rock. And the rain fell, and the floods came, and the winds blew and beat on that house, but it did not fall, because it had been founded on the rock. (Matthew 7:24-25)

IN THE MORNING

MAY 27TH

"THE TO-GO-PLATE"

What do you do when you have to give folks food to go? You provide them with a to-go plate.

The question is: How many plates are you NOT giving out?

See, there comes a time that you must give folks their food to go. Why? Because having them sit at your table can cause harm.

Remember, you can feed them, but they don't have to sit with you!!!!!!

"Blessed is the man who walks not in the counsel of the wicked, nor stands in the way of sinners, nor sits in the seat of scoffers; but his delight is in the law of the Lord, and on his law he meditates day and night." (Psalm 1:1-2)

In The Morning

_____
_____
_____
_____
_____
_____
_____
_____
_____
_____
_____

MAY 28TH

"TAKE IT OR LEAVE IT"

Has someone ever told you: Take it or leave it! And you decided to take it.

So often, when that question is raised, folks usually take it. But at what cost?

Remember, if they give you an ultimatum, be smart and LEAVE IT!!!!!

"Walk away from the company of fools, for you cannot find insight in their words. It takes wisdom for the clever to understand the path they are on, but the fool is deceived by his own foolishness.' (Proverbs 14:7-8) (VOICE)

IN THE MORNING

_____

_____

_____

_____

_____

_____

_____

_____

_____

_____

MAY 29ᵀᴴ

"ALL SNAKES DON'T HISS"

Snakes are nothing but long reptiles. And some of them have a venomous bite. The question is: What snakes are you around?

See, it's a knee-jerk reaction to say NO. Especially if you're not fond of serpents, but all snakes don't come in the form of reptiles.

Remember, snakes just don't hiss. Some walk around calling you friend, family, and colleague.

"Behold, I have given you authority to tread on serpents and scorpions, and over all the power of the enemy, and nothing shall hurt you." (Luke 10:19)

In The Morning

MAY 30TH

"THE PRESS RELEASE"

Press releases are official statements issued to the public. The question is: How many bulletins are you giving out?

See, everyone isn't happy for you. And every time you announce your next move. You're giving a press release.

Remember, some moves need to be made in silence!

"The wise don't tell everything they know, but the foolish talk too much and are ruined." (Proverbs 10:14)

In The Morning

MAY 31ST

"FROM A DISTANCE"

They did you wrong. And now they act as if nothing ever happened. Sound familiar?

See, there comes a time that you have to forgive. But that doesn't mean you have to forget.

Remember, there are some people you MUST love from a distance!!!!

"But to you who are willing to listen, I say, love your enemies! Do good to those who hate you. Bless those who curse you. Pray for those who hurt you." (Luke 6:27-28)

In The Morning

_____
_____
_____
_____
_____
_____
_____
_____
_____
_____
_____
_____
_____
_____

JUNE 1ST

"I'M TRANSITIONING"

When a person transitions, they go through a change process from one state to another, just like a caterpillar turning into a butterfly.

See, what you're going through might hurt like hell. But it's going to work out for your good. (Romans 8:28)

Remember, your storm is nothing more than you transitioning from one place to another.

IT IS WELL!!!!!

"Have I not commanded you? Be strong and courageous. Do not be frightened, and do not be dismayed, for the Lord your God is with you wherever you go." (Joshua 1:9)

In The Morning

_____

_____

_____

_____

_____

_____

_____

_____

_____

JUNE 2ND

"BUT YOU ALLOW IT"

When you allow something or someone to continue with what they're doing, you're giving them permission. The question is: What are you allowing?

See, there comes a time that you have to put your foot down. The fact that you keep talking and grumbling about it isn't helping your situation.

Remember, you can't keep complaining about what YOU allow!!!

"And don't complain as some of them did, and were killed by the destroyer." (1 Corinthians 10:10)

In The Morning

JUNE 3ᴿᴰ

"OVERTHINKING IT"

When a person overthinks, they think about (something) too much or for too long. The question is: What are you overthinking?

See, folks overload their mind with worry. And you can't keep stressing over something that you should've turned over to the Lord. (1 Peter 5:7)

Remember, either you're going to OVERCOME or OVERTHINK. But you can't do both!!!!

"For everyone born of God overcomes the world. This is the victory that has overcome the world, even our faith." (1 John 5:4)

In The Morning

_____
_____
_____
_____
_____
_____
_____
_____
_____
_____
_____

JUNE 4TH

"MAKING GOD LAUGH"

There's a saying that goes: "If you want to make God laugh, tell Him your plans." (Woody Allen) The question is: How many of you are making God laugh?

YES! You're supposed to write the vision down and run with it. But it doesn't mean that the road will be easy. (Habakkuk 2:2)

Remember, the hurt, pain, and betrayal are all part of God's plan. Jesus would've never seen the cross without Judas!!! (Matthew 26:15) & (Matthew 27:1–10)

"You can make many plans, but the LORD's purpose will prevail." (Proverbs 19:21)

In The Morning

_____
_____
_____
_____
_____
_____
_____
_____
_____
_____
_____
_____

JUNE 5TH

"IT'S NOT FROM GOD"

Whatever is good and perfect is a gift coming down to us from God our Father. (James 1:17) But what happens when your "gift" causes pure hell?

See, everything isn't from God. That's why you must put on the whole armor of God so that you will be able to withstand the tricks and schemes from the enemy. (Ephesians 6:11)

Remember, the enemy's job is to steal, kill and destroy. And if that's happening, it's NOT from God!!!! (John 10:10)

"Stay alert! Watch out for your great enemy, the devil. He prowls around like a roaring lion, looking for someone to devour." (1 Peter 5:8)

In The Morning

JUNE 6TH

"THEY DON'T WANT TO BE FIXED"

Do you know someone that needs help? But they're in denial of it. See, you can want others to be better all YOU want. But if they're not ready, there's nothing you can do about it.

Remember, STOP driving yourself crazy trying to fix others that don't see anything wrong with themselves!

"But understand this, that in the last days there will come times of difficulty. For people will be lovers of self, lovers of money, proud, arrogant, abusive, disobedient to their parents, ungrateful, unholy, heartless, unappeasable, slanderous, without self-control, brutal, not loving good, treacherous, reckless, swollen with conceit, lovers of pleasure rather than lovers of God, having the appearance of godliness, but denying its power. Avoid such people." (2 Timothy 3:1-5)

In The Morning

___
___
___
___
___
___
___
___
___

JUNE 7TH

"DON'T GO BLIND"

You wrote the vision and ran with it. But those around you can't see clearly. Sound familiar? (Habakkuk 2:2)

See, there's a cost to your circle. And some can hinder you from moving forward. (1 Corinthians 15:33)

Remember, if your circle has no vision, it can cause you to go blind!!!!

"Leave them; they are blind guides. If the blind lead the blind, both will fall into a pit." (Matthew 15:14)

In The Morning

_____
_____
_____
_____
_____
_____
_____
_____
_____
_____
_____
_____
_____
_____
_____

JUNE 8TH

"UNACCEPTABLE BEHAVIOR"

You've been taken blow by blow. And now you're ready to strike back. Sound familiar?

YES! You have every right to be upset and angry. But taking your frustration out on others that didn't even cause the pain is WRONG!!!

Remember, your pain can be understandable. So make sure your behavior is acceptable too!

"So get rid of all evil behavior. Be done with all deceit, hypocrisy, jealousy, and all unkind speech. Like newborn babies, you must crave pure spiritual milk so that you will grow into a full experience of salvation. Cry out for this nourishment," (1 Peter 2:1-2)

In The Morning

_____
_____
_____
_____
_____
_____
_____
_____
_____
_____
_____
_____

JUNE 9TH

"GETTING SAVED"

Whether it was a job loss or a relationship, the end of something can hurt, especially if you didn't end it.

I get it! You wanted it and didn't want it to end. But count it all joy. Because what you couldn't do, God allowed. (James 1:2-4)

Remember, there is no need to weep any longer. What you thought was a loss was you getting saved!!!!!

"You intended to harm me, but God intended it all for good. He brought me to this position so I could save the lives of many people." (Genesis 50:20)

In The Morning

_____
_____
_____
_____
_____
_____
_____
_____
_____
_____
_____
_____

JUNE 10TH

"PUT IT IN PARK"

Have you ever had to pick folks up in your car? And they get in and ride, but the whole time they're a disruption. Sound familiar?

See, that's how life can be. Some people are around you ONLY for the ride.

Remember, sometimes you have to PARK and not take them along with you!!!!

"The righteous should choose his friends carefully. For the way of the wicked leads them astray." (Proverbs 12:26)

IN THE MORNING

JUNE 11TH

"THE UGLY PART"

You can't stand it.
You wish it never happened.
You want it to go away.

Sound familiar?

See, that's what we call the "ugly part." And everyone has something that they think is ugly.

Whether it's part of their past or something on them that they don't like. To them, it isn't pleasant, and they want it gone.

Remember, even your ugliest part will catapult you to your destiny and testimony.

Beauty for ashes!!!!!!

"To all who mourn in Israel, he will give a crown of beauty for ashes, a joyous blessing instead of mourning, festive praise instead of despair. In their righteousness, they will be like great oaks that the LORD has planted for his own glory." (Isaiah 61:3)

In The Morning

_____
_____
_____
_____
_____
_____

JUNE 12TH

"RUNNING AWAY FROM YOURSELF"

When someone runs away, they leave and escape from a place, person, or situation of danger. But what happens when you're in the "situation"?

See, it's easy to escape from folks that cause you harm. But sometimes, the ones causing the most damage can be yourself.

Remember, everywhere you go in life, you have to take YOU with you. So STOP running away from yourself!!!!

"Examine yourselves to see whether you are in the faith; test yourselves. Can't you see for yourselves that Jesus Christ is in you—unless you actually fail the test?" (2 Corinthians 13:5)

In The Morning

JUNE 13TH

"IT'S WHAT I HAD"

It's incredible and one of the best things that you've ever had. But you don't appreciate it. Sound familiar?

See, it's easy to dismiss something that's always been there. But when you don't appreciate it, it can become a memory.

Remember, start appreciating what you HAVE before it becomes what you H.A.D.!

"Everything in the world is about to be wrapped up, so take nothing for granted. Stay wide-awake in prayer. Most of all, love each other as if your life depended on it. Love makes up for practically anything." (1 Peter 4:7-8)

In The Morning

_____
_____
_____
_____
_____
_____
_____
_____
_____
_____
_____
_____

JUNE 14TH

"I WANT THEIR LIFE"

They hate on you. But deep inside, they want to be like you.

See often; imitation can irritate the one being copied. But instead of getting irritated, be flattered.

Remember, many will want your life, but they can't handle the fight it takes!

"You want what you don't have, so you scheme and kill to get it. You are jealous of what others have, but you can't get it, so you fight and wage war to take it away from them. Yet you don't have what you want because you don't ask God for it." (James 4:2)

IN THE MORNING

_____
_____
_____
_____
_____
_____
_____
_____
_____
_____
_____
_____
_____

JUNE 15TH
"BE PICKY"

A peck of pickled peppers Peter Piper picked. If Peter Piper picked a peck of pickled peppers, where's the peck of pickled peppers Peter Piper picked? (John Harris 1813)

How many of you twisted up the rhyme?

See as cute as the tongue twister is. It's tricky and won't flow properly if you choose to rush it.

What am I saying? Your energy is sacrosanct!

So it doesn't matter how folks rhyme or flow. You have to BE PICKY about the energy that surrounds YOU!!

"But the Lord is faithful. He will establish you and guard you against the evil one." (2 Thessalonians 3:3)

IN THE MORNING

_____
_____
_____
_____
_____
_____
_____
_____
_____
_____

JUNE 16TH
"THE EXPOSE"

They confided in you. But you tell the friend that they're not friends with. Now surely that isn't you, is it?

See, you're not a friend when you break a trusted confidant, especially when they ask you to carry something that you can't wait to spill.

Remember, before you "expose" someone else's secrets. Think about all the times God's love for YOU covered your multitude of sins.

"Whoever slanders their neighbor in secret, I will put to silence; whoever has haughty eyes and a proud heart, I will not tolerate." (Psalm 101:5)

In The Morning

_____
_____
_____
_____
_____
_____
_____
_____
_____
_____
_____
_____

JUNE 17TH
"I NEED DIRECTIONS"

Have you ever been to a new place and got lost? So you ask a person that's not from there either, but they confuse you more. Sound familiar?

See, that's how life can be. Folks will ask for directions and help from others who don't know where they're going either.

Remember, STOP asking people who have never been where you're going for directions!!!!

"The LORD says, "I will guide you along the best pathway for your life. I will advise you and watch over you." (Psalm 32:8)

In The Morning

_____
_____
_____
_____
_____
_____
_____
_____
_____
_____
_____
_____

JUNE 18TH
"YOU MADE IT BEFORE THEM"

You were on cloud nine when you had them. Everything was great. But out of nowhere, they left. Sound familiar?

Yes! Things might be hard now. But no one said that the road would be easy. You've been here before, and you'll make it again. (Proverbs 18:24)

Remember, you made it before them, and you can make it without them! (Philippians 4:13)

"I know what it is to be in need, and I know what it is to have plenty. I have learned the secret of being content in any and every situation, whether well fed or hungry, whether living in plenty or in want." (Philippians 4:12)

IN THE MORNING

_____

_____

_____

_____

_____

_____

_____

_____

_____

_____

_____

_____

JUNE 19TH

"DON'T ANSWER"

Has someone ever called you and got you all worked up and agitated? Sound familiar?

See, your peace is priceless!!! And you shouldn't entertain anyone that's disturbing it..

Remember, just because they called doesn't mean you have to answer!!!!!

"Turn away from evil and do good; seek peace and pursue it." (Psalm 34:14)

In The Morning

_____
_____
_____
_____
_____
_____
_____
_____
_____
_____
_____
_____
_____
_____
_____

JUNE 20TH

"CLOCKS DON'T REWIND"

It's a part of your past, and now you want to go back in time. Sound familiar?

I get it! It's a part of the good ole days. Unfortunately, all good things must come to an end. (Philippians 3:12-14)

Remember, life is like a clock. It moves forward, not backwards.

"Remember not the former things, nor consider the things of old. Behold, I am doing a new thing; now it springs forth, do you not perceive it? I will make a way in the wilderness and rivers in the desert." (Isaiah 43:18-19)

In The Morning

_____
_____
_____
_____
_____
_____
_____
_____
_____
_____
_____
_____
_____
_____

JUNE 21ST

"S.O.S"

When someone is calling out for an urgent appeal for help, they signal S.O.S. The question is: How many of you are not signaling?

I get it! You don't want anyone to know, and you're prideful. But pride goes before destruction and a haughty spirit before fall. (Proverbs 16:18)

Remember, God doesn't care what you're dilemma is. He is your help!!! (Psalm 46:1-3)

"Let us then with confidence draw near to the throne of grace, that we may receive mercy and find grace to help in time of need." (Hebrews 4:16)

In The Morning

_____
_____
_____
_____
_____
_____
_____
_____
_____
_____
_____
_____

JUNE 22ND

"SAY NOTHING, DO NOTHING"

For no reason at all, they don't like you. Sound familiar?

See, favor isn't fair. And the reason some folks don't like you isn't because of what've you done.

It's the jealousy they have towards the blessings and favor on your life.

Remember, the best response for your enemy is to say and do NOTHING!!!!

"The LORD will fight for you, and you shall hold your peace." (Exodus 14:14)

IN THE MORNING

JUNE 23RD

"SOLID AS A ROCK"

Once a person crumbles, they break or fall apart into small fragments. And this happens over some time as part of a process of deterioration. The question is: What has you crumbling?

I get it! Life has hit you hard. But it doesn't mean that you won't come back from the hardships. (Psalm 18:2)

Remember, you're solid and built for what comes your way.

YOU WON'T CRUMBLE!!!!!

"We are hunted down, but never abandoned by God. We get knocked down, but we are not destroyed." (2 Corinthians 4:9)

In The Morning

_____
_____
_____
_____
_____
_____
_____
_____
_____
_____
_____
_____
_____

JUNE 24TH

"WORTHLESS TO PRICELESS"

When people are worthless, they feel they have no real value, purpose, or use. And it's usually because of the actions of someone or a result of something that happened. The question is: How many of you are currently feeling like that?

See, the enemy comes to steal, kill and destroy. And they can form weapons on you all day long. But it doesn't mean it will prosper. (John 10:10) (Isaiah 54:17)

Remember, never let someone define who you are. You're PRICELESS!!!

"Now this is what the LORD says—He who created you, O Jacob, and He who formed you, O Israel: "Do not fear, for I have redeemed you; I have called you by your name; you are Mine!" (Isaiah 43:1)

In The Morning

_____
_____
_____
_____
_____
_____
_____
_____
_____
_____
_____

JUNE 25TH

"BUT WHAT'S WRONG WITH YOU?"

Have you been quick to talk about everyone else's issues but won't say anything about yourself? Sound familiar?

See, it takes an immature person to sit and talk about everything wrong with other people. But they would never look in the mirror at themselves.

Remember, you become mature when you can see what's wrong in YOU and not others.

"Then we will no longer be immature like children. We won't be tossed and blown about by every wind of new teaching. We will not be influenced when people try to trick us with lies so clever they sound like the truth. Instead, we will speak the truth in love, growing in every way more and more like Christ, who is the head of his body, the church." (Ephesians 4:14-15)

In The Morning

_____
_____
_____
_____
_____
_____
_____
_____
_____
_____

JUNE 26TH

"OUCH! THAT HURTS"

Rejection hurts, and no one wants to be rejected. But sometimes, rejection is necessary.

See, sometimes God will remove what you can't get rid of on your own. Now that doesn't mean they're a terrible person. It's just that part of your story is coming to an end.

Remember, rejection boils down to three things: They're not good for you, not good TO YOU, or not GOOD for what God is doing IN YOU!!!!!

"As you come to him, the living Stone--rejected by humans but chosen by God and precious to him" (1 Peter 2:4)

In The Morning

_____
_____
_____
_____
_____
_____
_____
_____
_____
_____
_____
_____

JUNE 27TH

"GO STRESS OUT SOMEONE ELSE"

They've worked your last nerve. And just being around them has stressed you OUT! Sound familiar?

See, some folks mean you no good. And for the sake of your peace – it's your right to vacate.

Remember, sometimes, no explanation is needed. Just leave and let them go stress out someone else!!!

"Turn away from evil and do good; seek peace and pursue it." (Psalm 34:14)

In The Morning

_____
_____
_____
_____
_____
_____
_____
_____
_____
_____
_____
_____
_____
_____
_____

JUNE 28TH

"THEY DIDN'T CUT YOU"

Has someone hurt you to the core? And now you treat everyone like they caused your wound. Sound familiar?

See (everyone) didn't hurt you. And it's wrong to punish all for what O.N.E. person did.

Remember, if you're not careful, you'll end up bleeding on folks that didn't even cut you!

"Let all bitterness and wrath and anger and clamor and slander be put away from you, along with all malice. Be kind to one another, tenderhearted, forgiving one another, as God in Christ forgave you." (Ephesians 4:31-32)

In The Morning

_____
_____
_____
_____
_____
_____
_____
_____
_____
_____
_____

JUNE 29TH

"I GREW UP"

You've grown and moved on. But folks from your past only remember the old you. Sound familiar?

See, sometimes people can't accept the new you. And that doesn't mean you go back to your old ways to suit their needs either.

Remember, if folks want to see the old you. Tell them you don't exist anymore.

"When I was a child, I spoke and thought and reasoned as a child. But when I grew up, I put away childish things." (1 Corinthians 13:11)

In The Morning

_____

_____

_____

_____

_____

_____

_____

_____

_____

_____

_____

_____

JUNE 30TH
"I DON'T HAVE IT FIGURED OUT"

Stressed, worried, and trying to figure out what to do. Sound familiar?

I get it! You're getting attacked from every side, and it's too much to bear. But it's okay if you don't know what to do.

Remember, YOU don't have to have it all together - God does. Just make sure you turn your worries over to Him.

"Cast all your anxiety on Him, because He cares for you." (1 Peter 5:7)

In The Morning

JULY 1ST

"DILUTING YOURSELF"

When you want to dilute (something), you're making it weaker in force by modifying it or adding other elements to it. The question is: Are you diluting yourself?

See, it's a knee-jerk reaction to say NO. But you do if you keep watering down your gifts because of other folks' insecurities.

Remember, once you completely HEAL and become FREE. You'll STOP diluting yourself!!!

"It is for freedom that Christ has set us free. Stand firm, then, and do not be encumbered once more by a yoke of slavery." (Galatians 5:1)

In The Morning

_____
_____
_____
_____
_____
_____
_____
_____
_____
_____
_____
_____

JULY 2ND

"THIS IS IT"

Have you ever wanted something to come to an end, but you don't have the courage to do it? So you wait for the other person to call it quits. Sound familiar?

See, there comes a time that YOU have to decide: THIS IS IT! And waiting on someone else to determine what you already have the answer for can cost you.

Remember, your situation won't end by itself. YOU must end it!!!

"For there is a proper time and procedure for every matter, though a person may be weighed down by misery." (Ecclesiastes 8:6)

IN THE MORNING

JULY 3RD
"THE NEXT MOVE IS ON YOU"

They told you they were sorry. You said you forgive them. But you're still sour about what happened. Sound familiar?

See, when someone wrongs you, it can hurt. But sometimes, the folks that do you dirty won't apologize. So when they do, you must forgive them.

Remember, the next move is on YOU. But if you won't forgive them, you will be the one still hurting.

"Get rid of all bitterness, rage, anger, harsh words, and slander, as well as all types of evil behavior. Instead, be kind to each other, tenderhearted, forgiving one another, just as God through Christ has forgiven you." (Ephesians 4:31-32)

In The Morning

_____
_____
_____
_____
_____
_____
_____
_____
_____
_____

JULY 4TH

"CEASE AND DESIST"

When someone gives you a (Cease and Desist) letter, it's for you to stop doing your illegal activity and not starting it up again. In other words: You've Been Warned!

The question is: How many letters have you given out, and do you owe yourself one too?

See, it's easy to call out others for what they're doing. But at what point do you do your self-check?

Remember, before you warn someone else. Make sure you're not doing the same thing!

"Besides, they will become lazy and get into the habit of going from house to house. Next, they will start gossiping and become busybodies, talking about things that are none of their business." (1 Timothy 5:13)

IN THE MORNING

_____
_____
_____
_____
_____
_____
_____
_____

JULY 5TH

"I'M BREAKING"

Growing takes you through a process of increasing in physical size. The question is: Can you endure the process?

See, the answer is YES! Why? Because YOU ARE still GROWING while GOING through the suffering.

Remember, growing might feel like breaking at first.

"But the one who endures to the end will be saved." (Matthew 24:13)

In The Morning

JULY 6TH

"EVERYBODY CAN'T TELL THE SAME LIE"

Everywhere you go, there's a problem. But you say: It's not YOU, it's them. Sound familiar?

See, it's easy to see faults in others. But you have to look in the mirror at yourself too.

Remember, everybody can't tell the same lie, and everything isn't the enemy.

Sometimes it's the INNER YOU!!!!

"For if anyone thinks he is something, when he is nothing, he deceives himself." (Galatians 6:3)

In The Morning

_____
_____
_____
_____
_____
_____
_____
_____
_____
_____
_____
_____
_____
_____

JULY 7TH

"FULL PANIC MODE"

You keep stressing about what to do. And before you know it - you're in FULL panic mode. Sound familiar?

See, you can make yourself have a panic attack with worry and stress. When God says you need to turn your cares over to Him. (1 Peter 5:7)

Remember, STOP overstressing the situation and invite God into it.

"Do not be anxious about anything, but in everything by prayer and supplication with thanksgiving let your requests be made known to God." (Philippians 4:6)

In The Morning

JULY 8TH

"WRONG AS TWO LEFT SHOES"

When you want to get a pair of shoes, you get a right and a left one. But what happens when you get two lefts? One isn't going to fit.

See, that's how life can be. We try to force things that we know don't fit.

So STOP being wrong, like two left shoes. If it's God's purpose, it will fit perfectly.

NO struggling, NO pain, and NO forcing!!!

"Therefore do not be foolish, but understand what the will of the Lord is." (Ephesians 5:17)

In The Morning

_____
_____
_____
_____
_____
_____
_____
_____
_____
_____
_____
_____

JULY 9TH

"GET RID OF YOUR PACIFIER"

Pacifiers are for babies as something to suck on, which typically keeps them from crying. But have you ever thought about the pacifiers adults use also?

See, folks try to pacify one another. And it usually happens when they keep the truth from them. When TRUTH is what they need to be set free. (John 8:32)

Remember, sometimes it's not good to pacify others' feelings. You have to speak TRUTH and LIFE even if it hurts.

"Let your conversation be always full of grace, seasoned with salt, so that you may know how to answer everyone." (Colossians 4:6)

In The Morning

JULY 10TH

"ACCESS DENIED"

They said they're sorry. You forgave them. But they still want access to your life. Sound familiar?

See, you're supposed to forgive folks that do you wrong. Now that doesn't mean you forget what they did. But you're choosing to FORGIVE instead.

Remember, just because you forgive them doesn't mean they should continue to have access to your life. (Proverbs 13:20)

"Bearing with one another and, if one has a complaint against another, forgiving each other; as the Lord has forgiven you, so you also must forgive." (Colossians 3:13)

In The Morning

_____
_____
_____
_____
_____
_____
_____
_____
_____
_____
_____
_____

JULY 11TH

"LETHAL TO MY HEART"

It looks good, and you desperately want it. But the question you have to ask: Is it good FOR me?

See whether it's food, candy, or someone you want to be with. ALL things aren't good for YOU. (Genesis 3: 1-4) (1 Peter 5:8)

Remember, it might be candy to your eyes, but LETHAL to your heart!

"Keep us from being tempted and protect us from evil." (Matthew 6:13)

In The Morning

JULY 12TH

"IT RAN ITS COURSE"

You loved it much. But it broke down on you. Sound familiar? See, there is a time and place for everything. And there are some people, places, and things that will run their course. (Ecclesiastes 3:1)

Remember, just because it broke down doesn't mean you have to have a breakdown too. (Ecclesiastes 7:14)

"A time to cry and a time to laugh. A time to grieve and a time to dance." (Ecclesiastes 3:4)

In The Morning

_____
_____
_____
_____
_____
_____
_____
_____
_____
_____
_____
_____
_____
_____
_____

JULY 13TH

"WILL IT EVER COME?"

You want it and prayed about it. Yet nothing is happening. Sound familiar?

See, it's a knee-jerk reaction to want it now. But just because you want it on your time doesn't mean that it's God's time. (Psalm 27:14)

Remember, you may be delayed in your plans, but you are NEVER denied with God on your side.

"For still the vision awaits its appointed time; it hastens to the end—it will not lie. If it seems slow, wait for it; it will surely come; it will not delay." (Habakkuk 2:3)

In The Morning

_____

_____

_____

_____

_____

_____

_____

_____

_____

_____

_____

JULY 14TH

"REPEATED LESSONS"

Have you ever gone through something traumatic? But you made it through, only to be back in the same situation again.

See, life has a way of repeating itself until you learn. And as bad as you don't want to see it again - You WILL until you master your lesson.

Remember, your time is sacrosanct. So don't spend it repeating the same lessons.

"Like a dog that returns to his vomit is a fool who repeats his folly." (Proverbs 26:11)

In The Morning

JULY 15TH

"YOU WERE TOLD NOT TOO"

You were told not to touch it. But you did it anyway, and now you have a burn. Sound familiar?

See, you're the ONLY one to blame for the choices and decisions YOU make. The truth is when you know better, you do better.

Remember, STOP making the same choices, then acting surprised by the outcome!

"Whoever conceals their sins does not prosper, but the one who confesses and renounces them finds mercy." (Proverbs 28:13)

In The Morning

_____
_____
_____
_____
_____
_____
_____
_____
_____
_____
_____
_____
_____
_____
_____
_____

JULY 16TH

"FACE IT: YOU WERE WRONG"

You were adamant about proving your point and being right. But you ended up being wrong. Sound familiar?

See, no one wants to advocate for something and be wrong. But when you are, you must face it and own it.

Remember, sometimes you need to swallow your pride and accept that you were wrong!!!

"Arise! For this matter is your responsibility, but we will be with you; be courageous and act." (Ezra 10:4)

In The Morning

_____
_____
_____
_____
_____
_____
_____
_____
_____
_____
_____
_____
_____
_____
_____

JULY 17TH

"D.E.P.R.E.S.S.I.O.N"

Depression is a severe mood disorder that will affect you immensely when you're enduring it. The question many ask is: Will this ever end?

The answer is YES! See, it might seem as if your whole world has been turning upside down. But your current situation isn't your final destination.

Remember, you can turn your depression upside down by rearranging your thoughts and changing the words to I PRESS ON!!!!!!

"I press on toward the goal for the prize of the upward call of God in Christ Jesus." (Philippians 3:14)

In The Morning

_____
_____
_____
_____
_____
_____
_____
_____
_____
_____
_____

JULY 18TH

"A TOUGH DECISION"

Tough decisions are hard but necessary. The question you have to ask yourself is: Can you do it?

See, no one wants to be put in a corner and have the weight of the world on them. But there's a cost when you can't do it.

Remember, there will be times that you have to make tough decisions that will hurt. But it can also be a blessing in disguise. (Proverbs 3:5-6)

"I can do nothing on my own. As I hear, I judge, and my judgment is just, because I seek not my own will but the will of him who sent me." (John 5:30)

In The Morning

___
___
___
___
___
___
___
___
___
___
___
___

JULY 19TH

"ALLERGIC TO THE TRUTH"

You've been living a lie for so long that the truth doesn't seem real anymore. Now surely that isn't YOU, is it?

See, some folks are allergic to the truth. Meaning that no matter how much you tell them their TRUTH, they can't handle it.

Remember, before the truth sets you free. You must recognize the lie that's holding you hostage!

"You will know the truth, and the truth will set you free." (John 8:32)

In The Morning

JULY 20TH

"WALLS UP (A DETACHED HEART)"

Your heart was broken, but you said you were healed. But you're too detached from opening up. Sound familiar?

See, a hardened heart is a natural defense against the pain of life. But some think because their heart is detached, it doesn't make it hardened. FALSE!

Remember, you can't confuse a detached heart with a healed one. Walls up doesn't make your heart heal!!!

"I pray that your hearts will be flooded with light so that you can understand the confident hope He has given to those He called—His holy people who are His rich and glorious inheritance." (Ephesians 1:18)

In The Morning

JULY 21ST

"TRAUMA BOND"

You say you're in love. But it's causing you hell and misery. In other words: It's your (trauma bond) Sound familiar?

See, love is patient and kind. But it's not hatred and evil. (1 Corinthians 13:4-7) And unfortunately, some folks can't tell the difference between their trauma and love.

Remember, trauma bond isn't love!!!!

"For the weapons of our warfare are not of the flesh but have divine power to destroy strongholds." (2 Corinthians 10:4)

In The Morning

_____
_____
_____
_____
_____
_____
_____
_____
_____
_____
_____
_____
_____
_____
_____

JULY 22ND

"NOT DEFEATED BY THE LOSS"

No one wants to lose. But sometimes, your loss is a win.

See, most people think because they win they're automatically victorious. But winners aren't the only ones that are champions.

Remember, victors aren't the people that never lose. They're the ones that were NEVER DEFEATED by the loss.

"But as for you, be strong and do not give up, for your work will be rewarded." (2 Chronicles 15:7)

In The Morning

_____
_____
_____
_____
_____
_____
_____
_____
_____
_____
_____
_____
_____
_____
_____
_____

JULY 23RD

"FORGIVENESS DOESN'T MEAN RESTORATION"

They hurt you; you said you forgive them. But they want to stay in your life. Sound familiar?

See, some folks are just toxic. And no matter how many times they say they're sorry and you forgive them. It doesn't mean that they have to be in your life.

Remember, forgiveness doesn't mean restoration. Your peace is PRICELESS!!!!

"And the peace of God, which surpasses all understanding, will guard your heart and your mind in Christ Jesus." (Philippians 4:7)

In The Morning

_____
_____
_____
_____
_____
_____
_____
_____
_____
_____
_____
_____
_____
_____

JULY 24TH

"LIVING BEYOND THE PAST"

You've gone through pure hell. Never did you think you'll be in a good place. Sound familiar?

See, the enemy's job is to kill and destroy. And what you went through almost took you out. But rejoice!!! Because you're STILL STANDING, and you're STILL HERE!!! (John 10:10) (Romans 5:3-5)

Remember, you're living beyond your past, and that's a good place.

"And after you have suffered a little while, the God of all grace, who has called you to his eternal glory in Christ, will himself restore, confirm, strengthen, and establish you." (1 Peter 5:10)

In The Morning

_____
_____
_____
_____
_____
_____
_____
_____
_____
_____
_____
_____
_____
_____

JULY 25TH

"IT'S NOT WHAT YOU WANT TO HEAR"

You said you wanted help. But you didn't like the support that you got. Sound familiar?

See, HELP can hurt when it's not what you wanted to hear. But what's going to help you might just hurt.

Remember, sometimes, what you NEED isn't what you want. But it will make you better!

"Listen to the words of the wise; apply your heart to my instruction." (Proverbs 22:17)

In The Morning

JULY 26TH

"GET OUT OF YOUR OWN WAY"

Has someone ever tried to block your way? But what happens when you're the person blocking it. Sound familiar?

See, a lot of times, you can't move forward because of yourself. And until you realize YOU'RE the one in the way. You'll stay STUCK.

Remember, get out of your WAY and let God work!

"Trust in the Lord with all your heart, and do not lean on your own understanding. In all your ways acknowledge Him, and He will make straight your paths." (Proverbs 3:5-6)

IN THE MORNING

___
___
___
___
___
___
___
___
___
___
___
___
___
___
___
___

JULY 27TH

"OUT OF THE COCOON"

Cocoons are a protective seal that butterflies stay in until they have completely transformed. The question is: When are you going to get out of your cocoon?

See, you might be thinking you're not a butterfly, so this doesn't apply to you. But it does if you're hiding from what you KNOW you should be doing.

Remember, the transformation will feel uncomfortable after you've spent years in hiding. But going back into your cocoon isn't an option!!!!

SOAR!!!!

"So, dear brothers and sisters, work hard to prove that you really are among those God has called and chosen. Do these things, and you will never fall away." (2 Peter 2:10)

In The Morning

_____

_____

_____

_____

_____

_____

_____

_____

JULY 28TH

"WIPE YOUR TEARS AND FACE"

You're sick and tired. But you're tired of being sick and tired. Sound familiar? (Jeremiah 45:3) (ESV)

YES! Throwing in the towel seems like an option. But you're NOT a quitter. This is why you must press on. (Philippians 3:14) (ESV)

Remember, every time you want to throw in the towel. Think about God throwing it back and saying: "Now wipe your tears and face and PRESS ON!!!!"

"For His anger is but for a moment, His favor is for a lifetime; Weeping may last for the night, But a shout of joy comes in the morning." (Psalm 30:5) (NASB)

In The Morning

_____
_____
_____
_____
_____
_____
_____
_____
_____
_____
_____

JULY 29TH

"PERFECT TIME"

You've been praying and waiting, yet nothing is happening, and now you're getting frustrated. Sound familiar?

See, just because you want it NOW. It doesn't mean that it's time for you to get it.

Remember, you have your time, and God has His. And His time is PERFECT!

Be still and wait!!!!

"Be patient, then, brothers and sisters, until the Lord's coming. See how the farmer waits for the land to yield its valuable crop, patiently waiting for the autumn and spring rains. You too, be patient and stand firm, because the Lord's coming is near." (James 5:7-8) (NIV)

In The Morning

_____
_____
_____
_____
_____
_____
_____
_____
_____

JULY 30TH

"IT'S NOT ABOUT WHAT HAPPENED TO YOU"

They lied to you.

They left you to die.

Because of them, you lost it all.

Sound familiar?

See, in life, things are going to happen to you. And, understandably, you want to wallow in the despair. But it's how you respond to it that matters. (Proverbs 15:1) (ESV)

Remember, it doesn't feel or look well. But you MUST RESPOND WELL to it!!!!

"Though He slay me, yet will I trust Him." (Job 13:15) (NKJV)

In The Morning

_____
_____
_____
_____
_____
_____
_____
_____
_____
_____

JULY 31ST

"YOU HAVE THE ANSWER TO THE PROBLEM"

Problems are something that no one wants to have. But everyone will experience them throughout their lives. The question is: What do you do when issues arise?

See, the difference between your answer and your problem lies within your feelings. And you're NOT how you feel, but you are what you think.

So start changing how you THINK, and you can change how you feel.

"Don't copy the behavior and customs of this world, but let God transform you into a new person by changing the way you think. Then you will learn to know God's will for you, which is good and pleasing and perfect." (Romans 12:2)

IN THE MORNING

_____

_____

_____

_____

_____

_____

_____

_____

_____

_____

AUGUST 1ST

"NOT MAD, JUST DONE!"

You're mad; they're angry, and yet you're getting nowhere with a resolution. Sound familiar?

See, peace is priceless. And going back and forth arguing with someone can cost you yours.

Remember, sometimes you have to quit being mad and just be DONE!!!!

"So get rid of all evil behavior. Be done with all deceit, hypocrisy, jealousy, and all unkind speech." (1 Peter 2:1)

In The Morning

_____
_____
_____
_____
_____
_____
_____
_____
_____
_____
_____
_____
_____
_____
_____
_____

AUGUST 2ND

"I'M STARVING"

When one is starving, they're suffering or dying from hunger. And that's how folks get when they get impatient.

See, when you're hungry, you want something NOW. And sometimes you'll take what's ready, instead of waiting for what you really want to be cooked.

What do I mean?

STOP letting your hunger cause you to take what's ready - versus what's being prepared for YOU!

"Be patient, then, brothers and sisters, until the Lord's coming. See how the farmer waits for the land to yield its valuable crop, patiently waiting for the autumn and spring rains. You too, be patient and stand firm, because the Lord's coming is near." (James 5:7-8) (NIV)

IN THE MORNING

_____

_____

_____

_____

_____

_____

_____

_____

AUGUST 3ᴿᴰ

"PRIVACY IS POWER"

Nowadays, when folks get exciting news, they can't wait to share it. And with various social media platforms, they immediately flock on them to spill their guts. So the question is, does that describe you?

See, there is nothing wrong with sharing details of your life. But it would be best if you were cautious with things you share.

Remember, privacy is power. And what people don't know they can't ruin.

"Better is a handful of quietness than two hands full of toil and a striving after wind." (Ecclesiastes 4:6)

In The Morning

___
___
___
___
___
___
___
___
___
___
___
___
___

AUGUST 4TH

"IS (IT) YOU?"

Have you ever been irritated because you want something to change?

See, it's a knee-jerk reaction to think it's the situation that's the problem when it could be YOU.

Remember, sometimes it's "YOU" that needs to change more than the "IT."

"Now it's time to change your ways! Turn to face God so he can wipe away your sins, pour out showers of blessing to refresh you, (Acts 3:19) (MSG)

In The Morning

_____
_____
_____
_____
_____
_____
_____
_____
_____
_____
_____
_____
_____

AUGUSTS 5TH

"I DIDN'T SEE IT COMING"

Have you ever seen a storm coming? But what about the ones that you have no clue that are on the horizon.

See, there will be things that happen to you that you won't see coming in life. The important thing is not to panic because the surprise catches you.

Remember, you may not have seen it coming, but God did. And He's prepared for it.

IT IS WELL!!!!

"Beloved, do not be surprised at the fiery trial when it comes upon you to test you, as though something strange were happening to you. But rejoice insofar as you share Christ's sufferings, that you may also rejoice and be glad when his glory is revealed." (1 Peter 4:12-13)

In The Morning

_____

_____

_____

_____

_____

_____

_____

_____

AUGUST 6TH

"IN RECOVERY"

When one is trying to recover, they're trying to return to a normal state of health, mind, or strength. And in some cases, they're regaining possession or control of what was taken.

The question is: Are you in recovery?

See, you might be thinking no because you're not back to your original state. But just because you haven't gotten to where you want to be, doesn't mean you're not in recovery.

Remember, some things are hard to recover from, but your recovery is necessary!!!!

"And after you have suffered a little while, the God of all grace, who has called you to his eternal glory in Christ, will himself restore, confirm, strengthen, and establish you." (1 Peter 5:10)

In The Morning

_____
_____
_____
_____
_____
_____
_____
_____
_____

AUGUST 7ᵀᴴ

"ENEMY LINES"

You were friends with them. But because of a dispute, you separated. And now the other party thinks the two of you are enemies. Sound familiar?

See it doesn't matter if it's family, friends, or colleagues. You can have disagreements with others and not draw enemy lines.

Remember, just because the relationship is over doesn't mean either of you should gain an enemy!

"Love your enemies! Do good to them. Lend to them without expecting to be repaid. Then your reward from heaven will be very great, and you will truly be acting as children of the Most High, for He is kind to those who are unthankful and wicked." (Luke 6:35)

In The Morning

_____
_____
_____
_____
_____
_____
_____
_____
_____
_____
_____
_____
_____

AUGUST 8TH

"AN OVERRIDE"

When you have to override something, you're interrupting what's taking place to take control. The question is: What things do you need to override?

See, life has a way of coming at you with a vengeance. And sometimes you're going to feel scared about the unknown. But God doesn't give us a spirit of fear. (2 Timothy 1:7)

Remember, let your FAITH override your fear when uncertain times come.

"Be joyful in hope, patient in affliction, faithful in prayer." (Romans 12:12)

In The Morning

_____
_____
_____
_____
_____
_____
_____
_____
_____
_____
_____
_____

AUGUST 9TH

"STOP THE TEMPER TANTRUMS"

Temper tantrums are something that generally children do. But have you ever thought about the tantrums adults encounter?

See, in life, things aren't going to go your way. And it shouldn't be a knee-jerk reaction to pop and go off.

Remember, we as believers must learn to operate in FAITH. God doesn't respond to our emotions; He responds to our FAITH.

"My dear brothers and sisters, take note of this: Everyone should be quick to listen, slow to speak and slow to become angry, because human anger does not produce the righteousness that God desires." (James 1:19-20)

In The Morning

AUGUST 10TH

"FROM BAD TO WORSE"

When things are bad, they're bad. But when the state or condition goes to an even worse shape. The question becomes: What can go wrong next?

See, no one wants to continue to go through storms back to back. But the rain won't last forever.

Remember, things might go from bad to worse. But YOU have to make sure you don't give up.

"Let us not grow weary in well-doing, for in due time we will reap a harvest, if we do not give up." (Galatians 6:9)

In The Morning

AUGUST 11TH

"INTENTIONAL SILENCE"

They said something to you. And now you want the last word. Sound familiar?

Lao Tzu says it best: Silence is a source of great strength. And the truth is, everything doesn't need a response.

Remember, there is POWER in intentional silence.

"Oh that you would keep silent, and it would be your wisdom!" (Job 13:5)

In The Morning

AUGUST 12ᵀᴴ

"BE YOUR OWN CHEERLEADER"

You're excited. But they could care less.

Sound familiar?

See, everyone isn't going to be happy for you. So there's no need to get upset and frustrated - because they don't share in your joy.

Remember, be your own cheerleader. Cheer for yourself, even when others won't.

"David was greatly distressed because the men were talking of stoning him; each one was bitter in spirit because of his sons and daughters. But David found strength in the LORD his God." (1 Samuel 30:6)

In The Morning

_____
_____
_____
_____
_____
_____
_____
_____
_____
_____
_____
_____

AUGUST 13TH

"FIGHT OR FLIGHT"

Some folks FIGHT because it's what is in them. And others FLIGHT because they get scared. The question is: Which are you?

See, it's a stance that you must take when adversity strikes. And just because you're scared doesn't mean you should run. (2 Timothy 1:7)

Remember, decide to FIGHT the good fight with FAITH. And God will handle the rest. (Deuteronomy 20:4)

"Fight the good fight for the true faith. Hold tightly to the eternal life to which God has called you, which you have declared so well before many witnesses." (1 Timothy 6:12)

In The Morning

___
___
___
___
___
___
___
___
___
___
___
___
___

AUGUST 14TH

"GET YOUR PRIORITIES STRAIGHT"

Have you ever had the attitude of, "I'll get around to it when I feel like it?"

See, it's easy to put things in second and third place. But the question is: How would you feel if God did you like that?

In other words, STOP dissing what YOU need. (God)

It's time to get your priorities straight!

"Seek the Kingdom of God above all else, and live righteously, and He will give you everything you need." (Matthew 6:33)

In The Morning

_____
_____
_____
_____
_____
_____
_____
_____
_____
_____
_____
_____
_____

AUGUST 15TH

"THE DEVASTATION"

When a person is devastated, they have a severe and overwhelming shock or grief. The question is: How do you handle your disappointments?

Unfortunately, the devastation is a gut punch to the core. And as much as it hurts, God will use it for your good. (Romans 8:28)

Remember, you might not have seen it coming. But God did. And a little hurt now is much better than a big hurt later!!!!

"Praise be to the God and Father of our Lord Jesus Christ, the Father of compassion and the God of all comfort, who comforts us in all our troubles, so that we can comfort those in any trouble with the comfort we ourselves receive from God." (2 Corinthians 1:3-4)

In The Morning

_____

_____

_____

_____

_____

_____

_____

_____

_____

_____

_____

_____

_____

AUGUST 16TH

"IF THE SHOE FITS WEAR IT"

Everybody keeps telling you the same thing. But you're stuck in denial. Now surely that isn't YOU.

The truth is everyone can't tell the same lie. And if something applies to you. Eventually, it will be at a cost when you don't own it.

Remember, if the shoe fits, wear it!!!

STOP being in denial!

"Arise, for it is your task, and we are with you; be strong and do it." (Ezra 10:4)

In The Morning

_____
_____
_____
_____
_____
_____
_____
_____
_____
_____
_____
_____
_____

AUGUST 17TH

"A BULLET DODGED"

You wanted it badly. And the fact it didn't happen has left you heartbroken. Sound familiar?

See, there are things in life that you want. But God doesn't want for you.

And what you don't have the sense to STOP, He will.

Remember, some heartaches are due from the graze of the bullet dodged!

"The LORD keeps you from all harm and watches over your life." (Psalm 121:7)

In The Morning

AUGUST 18TH

"IT'S EVERYTHING THAT YOU EVER WANTED (IN DISGUISED)"

On the outside, you thought they were sweet and lovable. But you couldn't see they were raging wolves underneath. Sound familiar?

See, the enemy comes to steal, kill and destroy. (John 10:10) This is why you MUST put on the whole armor of God to withstand his tricks and schemes. (Ephesians 6:11-18)

Remember, your adversary isn't going to come as you think. They will enter dressed as everything you've ever wanted. (Matthew 7:15)

"Stay alert! Watch out for your great enemy, the devil. He prowls around like a roaring lion, looking for someone to devour." (1 Peter 5:8)

In The Morning

_____

_____

_____

_____

_____

_____

_____

_____

AUGUST 19TH

"EVERY BATTLE ISN'T PUBLIC"

Folks all over the world are going through things. But just because you don't know about it. That doesn't mean they don't have a battle.

See, everyone in life has problems. Now their trials might be different from yours. But they still exist.

Remember, every battle isn't public. So be kind when treating others.

The truth is, you don't know WHAT they're going through!!!!

"This is my commandment, that you love one another as I have loved you." (John 15:12)

In The Morning

___
___
___
___
___
___
___
___
___
___
___
___
___
___

AUGUST 20TH
"LIFE GOES ON"

Disaster has a way of striking when you at least expect it—leaving one to ask: "What now?

See, it's a knee-jerk reaction to want to give up. But you can't! And it's at that moment when you must decide to press on. (Galatians 6:9)(Philippians 3:14)

Remember, life goes on and you have to go with it!!!!

"I have said these things to you, that in me you may have peace. In the world you will have tribulation. But take heart; I have overcome the world." (John 16:33)

In The Morning

AUGUST 21ST

"THROWN IN THE FIERY FURNACE"

You've been thrown into the fiery furnace. And you're questioning God as to why He isn't helping you. Sound familiar?

See, God has a plan for ALL things. And just because you don't know the answer to it. That doesn't mean He doesn't know what He's doing. (Jeremiah 29:11) (Romans 8:28)

Remember, there are times that God won't stop you from being thrown in the fire. Why? Because He has a point to prove to those who threw you in!!!

"When you pass through the waters, I will be with you; and when you go through the rivers, they will not overwhelm you. When you walk through the fire, you will not be scorched, and the flames will not set you ablaze." (Isaiah 43:2)

In The Morning

_____
_____
_____
_____
_____
_____
_____
_____
_____
_____

AUGUST 22ND

"THE PEW WARMERS"

They're the ones that go to church every Sunday. Site scriptures after one another. And they seem as if they never do anything wrong. But that's not YOU, is it?

See, some sheep come in wolves' clothing. And being a pew warmer on Sundays doesn't mean you're "right." (Matthew 7:15)

Remember, the devil at one point lived in Heaven too. And he wasn't right!!!! (Revelation 12:7-12) (Isaiah 14:12)

"Now there were also false prophets among the people, just as there will be false teachers among you. They will secretly introduce destructive heresies, even denying the Master who bought them—bringing swift destruction on themselves." (2 Peter 2:1)

In The Morning

_____
_____
_____
_____
_____
_____
_____
_____
_____
_____
_____
_____

AUGUST 23ᴿᴰ

"THE DRAGGING CONTEST"

(They) were talking about them. And you were listening. Sound familiar?

See, there are times that YOU might be a witness to a dragging contest. And that's when a bunch of folks get around and gossip to drag others through the mud.

Now you might not say anything wrong or join in. But what does it say about you for listening and doing nothing?

Remember, be known to SHUT DOWN conversations that focus on tearing others to pieces.

"Let no unwholesome talk come out of your mouths, but only what is helpful for building up the one in need and bringing grace to those who listen." (Ephesians 4:29)

In The Morning

_____

_____

_____

_____

_____

_____

_____

_____

_____

AUGUST 24ᵀᴴ

"PRIVATE INTEGRITY"

In public, they're all together. And everything that comes out of their mouth is politically correct. But the question is: "Are they the same behind closed doors?"

See, we live in a world now where everyone wants to be (Facebook) famous and (Instant) Instagram stars. And it's easy to post or showcase how you want others to see you. But if that's not who you really are, you're portraying a lie.

Remember, public success will require private integrity! (Proverbs 11:3)

"Whoever walks in integrity walks securely, but he who makes his ways crooked will be found out." (Proverbs 10:9)

In The Morning

AUGUST 25TH

"THE FORGIVEN ONES"

You did wrong, and they still forgave you. Sound familiar?

See when you do something that hurts someone else. You want forgiveness. But have you ever thought about the forgiveness you WON'T give to those that wronged you?

Remember, FORGIVEN folks need to be FORGIVING people!!!

"But if you do not forgive others their trespasses, neither will your Father forgive your trespasses." (Matthew 6:15)

In The Morning

AUGUST 26TH

"SECOND GUESSING YOURSELF"

It doesn't feel right. In your gut, you have a nauseating feeling about it. Sound familiar?

See, folks often second-guess what they already know the answer to; that's why you must abound in knowledge and discernment at all times. (Philippians 1:9-10)

Remember, STOP second-guessing yourself and trust the voice within!

"For the LORD grants wisdom! From his mouth come knowledge and understanding. He grants a treasure of common sense to the honest. He is a shield to those who walk with integrity. He guards the paths of the just and protects those who are faithful to him. Then you will understand what is right, just, and fair, and you will find the right way to go. For wisdom will enter your heart, and knowledge will fill you with joy. Wise choices will watch over you. Understanding will keep you safe. (Proverbs 2:6-11)

In The Morning

_____
_____
_____
_____
_____
_____
_____

AUGUST 27TH

"GETTING EVEN OR HAVING PEACE"

They hit you, so now you want to hit them back. Sound familiar? See, it's a knee-jerk reaction to want to go after the ones that have hurt you. But at what cost.

Remember, before you strike back, ask yourself: Do you want to get even, or do you want peace?

"Beloved, never avenge yourselves, but leave it to the wrath of God, for it is written, "Vengeance is mine, I will repay, says the Lord." (Romans 12:19)

In The Morning

AUGUST 28TH

"YOU'RE GIVING ME A HEADACHE"

Mean. Surly. Unkind. Angry. Now surely those words don't describe you, do they?

See, life might have thrown you some nasty blows. But it doesn't give you the right to take your frustration out on others.

Remember, being bitter and mean-spirited will cause you to be a nuisance. And no one wants to be bothered with a headache!

"Refrain from anger and turn from wrath; do not fret--it leads only to evil. For those who are evil will be destroyed, but those who hope in the LORD will inherit the land." (Psalm 37:8-9)

In The Morning

AUGUST 29TH

"DON'T GIVE FEAR AN AUDIENCE"

When tragedy strikes, it's easy to succumb to fear. However, God doesn't give us a spirit of fear, but of power and a sound mind. (2 Timothy 1:7)

So, if you're feeling overwhelmed by fear and uncertainty, the question is, where is your focus?

Remember, fear has no audience when God is your focus.

"You will keep in perfect peace all who trust in you, all whose thoughts are fixed on you!" (Isaiah 26:3)

In The Morning

AUGUST 30TH

"BITTER ROOTS"

You said you were past it and had moved on. But deep inside, you're bitter. Sound familiar?

See, it's a dangerous thing to be bitter and be in denial about it too. Bitterness is the root of evil, and it leads to destruction.

Remember, STOP letting bitter roots grow within.

"See to it that no one falls short of the grace of God and that no bitter root grows up to cause trouble and defile many. (Hebrews 12:15)

In The Morning

AUGUST 31ST

"A DIAMOND IS STILL A DIAMOND"

"You're nothing." "You won't make it." "You're trash."

See, those are words surly folks say when they're insecure with themselves and project their hate upon you.

The truth is, it doesn't matter what folks call you; because you are who God says you are. (1 Peter 2:9)

Remember, diamonds don't stop being diamonds because others see them as rocks. They're still a treasure, and so are YOU!!!

"And the LORD has declared today that you are a people for his treasured possession, as he has promised you, and that you are to keep all his commandments," (Deuteronomy 26:18)

IN THE MORNING

SEPTEMBER 1ST

"REMAINING THE SAME"

They say they want to change. But they keep doing what they've always done. Surely that isn't YOU, is it?

See, it's one thing to say you need to do something. And it's another actually to DO IT!

Remember, if your attitude and character don't change or your heart transforms, then you will remain the same.

The choice is YOURS!!!!!

"Don't copy the behavior and customs of this world, but let God transform you into a new person by changing the way you think. Then you will learn to know God's will for you, which is good and pleasing and perfect." (Romans 12:2)

In The Morning

SEPTEMBER 2ND

"GROWTH OVER COMPANY"

You wanted to work on yourself and did. But when you looked up, no one was there to be found. Sound familiar?

See growth and elevation will often lead to isolation. And that's okay.

Because getting yourself together will have you lonely but NOT alone. (Joshua 1:9)

Remember, you have to choose GROWTH over company!!

"But when that which is perfect has come, then that which is in part will be done away." (1 Corinthians 13:10)

IN THE MORNING

SEPTEMBER 3RD

"COMMITTED TO YOUR EGO"

You've been put in charge of facilitating it. And you proudly support it. But due to new circumstances, you've been removed. Sound familiar?

See, it's easy to cheer and be all in when it's what you're over. But the question is: Are you still going to remain on the team when you're let go from it?

Remember, if you only support what you're in charge of, you've not committed to the work of God but your ego!

"Pride goes before destruction, and a haughty spirit before a fall." (Proverbs 16:18)

In The Morning

_____
_____
_____
_____
_____
_____
_____
_____
_____
_____
_____

SEPTEMBER 4TH

"REPERCUSSIONS OF BAD CHOICES"

Have you ever been under attack? Then, were reminded about the seeds you've sowed?

See, you reap what you sow. And a lot of times, folks are quick to say the enemy is causing their havoc. But they forget about what they did too. (Galatians 6:7)

Remember, what you're thinking is an attack from the enemy could be the repercussions of bad choices!

"My experience shows that those who plant trouble and cultivate evil will harvest the same." (Job 4:8)

IN THE MORNING

SEPTEMBER 5TH

"MEND IT OR END IT"

Have you ever had a spat with someone, and the both of you were too stubborn to say sorry?

See, some relationships are worth saving. Then others must cease and desist.

Remember, either the relationship needs to mend or end.

"Faithful are the wounds of a friend, But deceitful are the kisses of an enemy." (Proverbs 27:6)

In The Morning

SEPTEMBER 6TH

"YOU CAN'T LEARN THEIR LESSON"

You keep getting frustrated and agitated. And it's nothing to do with you, but it's the concern you have for someone else. Sound familiar?

See, as much as you want to keep someone from getting hurt, you can't. They have to want it for themselves too.

Remember, you can't take lessons that someone else is supposed to learn.

"Arise! For this matter is your responsibility, but we will be with you; be courageous and act." (Ezra 10:4)

In The Morning

SEPTEMBER 7TH

"COMPLIMENTED BUT NOT CORRECTED"

Positive Affirmations: "You're amazing!" Criticisms: "You need to get going!"

See, it's one thing to receive compliments and love it. I mean, who doesn't want to hear nice things about themselves. But the question is: Can you also take criticism and being corrected?

Remember, if you can be complimented and not corrected, you lack spiritual maturity!

"Like newborn babies, you must crave pure spiritual milk so that you will grow into a full experience of salvation. Cry out for this nourishment," (1 Peter 2:2)

In The Morning

SEPTEMBER 8TH

"PRAY BEFORE YOU GOSSIP"

They sit around and gossip and give an opinion about other folks. But go mute if the subject turns to them. Surely that's not you, is it?

See, it's easy to talk about others and give your dissertation. But let's not forget about the things ONLY you and God know about.

Remember, think before you speak, and pray before you gossip!

"Speaking rashly is like a piercing sword, but the tongue of the wise brings healing." (Proverbs 12:18)

In The Morning

SEPTEMBER 9TH

"I HAVE A PLAN"

Have you ever had to develop a plan B because you weren't sure about your first plan working out?

See, instead of you sitting there trying to figure it out. You should be giving it to God, who has already worked it out. (Psalm 139:16)

Remember, God never has to come up with multiple plans. It will ALWAYS be plan A.

"The LORD of hosts has sworn: "As I have planned, so shall it be, and as I have purposed, so shall it stand," (Isaiah 14:24)

In The Morning

SEPTEMBER 10TH

"CAN I GET SOME SUPPORT"

You've worked hard on it, and you proudly want to show it off. But when you looked up, no one was there to cheer you on.

See, often the support that you think you're going to get, you won't. And it has nothing to do with you. It's the jealousy and envy in them.

Remember, sometimes people won't support you publicly because they've talked about you privately. But don't worry, it's okay. Your endorsement comes from God, not people!

"I will make you into a great nation, and I will bless you; I will make your name great, and you will be a blessing." (Genesis 12:2)

In The Morning

_____
_____
_____
_____
_____
_____
_____
_____
_____
_____
_____
_____

SEPTEMBER 11TH

"IMITATING THE RESULTS"

Have you ever worked so hard for something and paid your dues for it, then someone comes along trying to imitate what you've done?

See, many want the results of what others do. But they don't realize the hell it took to get it.

Remember, everybody wants to try to imitate results. But few will try to imitate submission.

"Be imitators of me, as I am of Christ. Now I commend you because you remember me in everything and maintain the traditions even as I delivered them to you." (1 Corinthians 11:1-2)

In The Morning

SEPTEMBER 12TH

"THE PLACE OF REFERENCE"

When some people think about their past, they get happy. Then some can't stand the thought of remembering it.

See, the past is just that: It's the past. It happened; it's over, and now it's time to move on. (Isaiah 43:18-19)

Remember, the past is not a place of residence but a reference.

"Brothers and sisters, I do not consider myself yet to have taken hold of it. But one thing I do: Forgetting what is behind and straining toward what is ahead," (Philippians 3:13)

In The Morning

SEPTEMBER 13TH

"PAINTING A DIFFERENT PICTURE"

They showed you who they are. But you won't accept the truth. Sound familiar?

May Angelou said it best, "When people show you who they are BELIEVE THEM!"

I get it! You want it. But just because you want it, doesn't mean that God wants it for YOU.

Remember, when God shows you their true colors, you don't need to paint a different picture. It is what it is!

"You can't keep your true self hidden forever; before long you'll be exposed. You can't hide behind a religious mask forever; sooner or later the mask will slip, and your true face will be known." (Luke 12:2)

In The Morning

___
___
___
___
___
___
___
___
___
___

SEPTEMBER 14TH

"BUT IT'S KILLING YOU"

Have you ever loved something so much that you knew it wasn't good for you, but you kept indulging in it?

See, it doesn't matter if it's something you're eating or if it's something or someone in your life. The truth is, if it's harming you - it needs to GO!

Remember, it's possible to love what's killing you. And just because you love it, it doesn't mean you need it.

"No temptation has overtaken you that is not common to man. God is faithful, and He will not let you be tempted beyond your ability, but with the temptation He will also provide the way of escape, that you may be able to endure it." (1 Corinthians 10:13)

In The Morning

_____
_____
_____
_____
_____
_____
_____
_____
_____
_____
_____
_____
_____

SEPTEMBER 15TH

"FRUSTRATED & DISAPPOINTED"

You thought they had what you needed, but they left. And now you think you can't do it without them. Sound familiar?

See, you're worried and all up in arms about something you have no business being consumed with. Why? Because God's got YOU!!

Remember, the reason you're worried is that you're wondering if you will have what you need when you need it.

But anytime you expect other folks to meet your needs instead of God - You will ALWAYS be frustrated and disappointed.

"Our God gives you everything you need, makes you everything you're to be. You need to know, friends, that thanking God over and over for you is not only a pleasure; it's a must. We have to do it. Your faith is growing phenomenally; your love for each other is developing wonderfully. Why, it's only right that we give thanks." (2 Thessalonians 1:2-3)

IN THE MORNING

_____

_____

_____

_____

_____

_____

_____

_____

SEPTEMBER 16TH

"PRAYERS ANSWERED IN DISGUISED"

You prayed. You've even asked others to pray for you. Yet, NOTHING! How many can relate?

See, it's a frustrating thing when you feel like God isn't answering your prayers. But is He really not answering?

Remember, you can never think that God doesn't love you because He isn't giving you what you want. Unanswered prayers can be your prayers answered in disguise.

Have faith; God always knows what's best!!!!

"Before they call, I will answer; while they are yet speaking, I will hear." (Isaiah 65:24)

In The Morning

___
___
___
___
___
___
___
___
___
___
___
___

SEPTEMBER 17TH

"SAME SCRIPT - DIFFERENT CAST"

You know the book. You've read it before. And you know how it's going to end. So why do you keep reading it again and again?

See, maybe there is a part of you that thinks if you read it differently - it will magically have a new ending.

WRONG!!! Same book, different cast.

Remember, God, blesses you with new mercy every morning. So why keep repeating it with the same script? (Lamentations 3:22-23)

"Like a dog that returns to his vomit is a fool who repeats his folly." (Proverbs 26:11)

In The Morning

_____
_____
_____
_____
_____
_____
_____
_____
_____
_____
_____

SEPTEMBER 18TH

"BEING DISOBEDIENT"

When someone is disobedient, they refuse to obey rules to someone in authority. Now, is that you?

I get it! You want to do your own thing. And what you're doing is so small and insignificant – You think it's' not hurting anyone. But it just might, and at what cost?

Remember, you can't be disobedient to God, then be mad about the pain the disobedience causes.

"If you are willing and obedient, You shall eat the good of the land." (Isaiah 1:19)

In The Morning

SEPTEMBER 19TH

"DON'T LET YOUR EYES KEEP TALKING FOR YOU"

You see it. You want it. But you know you shouldn't get it. But you go for it anyways. Sound familiar?

See, that's the story for many folks. They have eyes bigger than one's stomach. And in the end - it can cost you a tummy ache.

Remember, your eyes can sometimes talk you into something that your heart knows isn't good for you.

"Stay alert! Watch out for your great enemy, the devil. He prowls around like a roaring lion, looking for someone to devour." (1 Peter 5:8)

In The Morning

SEPTEMBER 20TH

"GET OFF THE MERRY-GO-ROUND"

Have you ever been in a circle that you were comfortable with, so you stay in it no matter how dizzy it makes you?

See, your circle might be the only reason why you're in the cycle you're in. But now, it's time to starve your ring.

Remember, you can't break the cycle if you're still in it!

"To put off your old self, which belongs to your former manner of life and is corrupt through deceitful desires, and to be renewed in the spirit of your minds, and to put on the new self, created after the likeness of God in true righteousness and holiness." (Ephesians 4:22-24)

In The Morning

SEPTEMBER 21ST

"RUNNING AFTER WHAT LEFT"

They left you. They've gone away. Now what? Now, YOU move on!!!!

Okay, you didn't want it to end. But it did. So does that mean your life is over? NO!

See, God will remove people for your protection. And when He does, it's not for you to run after them. (Psalm 121:7-8)

Remember, some folks are only for a season in your life. And when they go - you have to let them GO!!!

"They went out from us, but they did not really belong to us. For if they had belonged to us, they would have remained with us; but their going showed that none of them belonged to us." (1 John 2:19)

IN THE MORNING

_____
_____
_____
_____
_____
_____
_____
_____
_____
_____

SEPTEMBER 22ND

"WHY ARE YOU PUTTING IT BACK ON?"

You removed it because it weighed you down. And now – you want to put it back on. But that's not you, is it?

See, many folks often complain about what's causing them pain. And when they release it, they often find themselves right back into the very thing that caused the discomfort in the first place.

Remember, you can't put back on the same chains that God broke off!!!!

"Let's break the chains that hold us back and throw off the ropes that tie us down." (Psalm 2:3)

In The Morning

SEPTEMBER 23RD

"STOP LETTING THEM TALK TO YOU INTO A NIGHTMARE"

You have a dream that you're excited about, and you want to tell your friend. But just like that - they kill it.

How many can relate?

See, some folks are dream snatchers. They can't help it. It's not you – it's them!

Remember, learn not to talk about your dreams to non-dreamers. Because before you know it, they will have talked you out of your dreams and talked you into a nightmare!

"Indeed, I am against those who prophesy false dreams," declares the LORD. "They tell them and lead my people astray with their reckless lies, yet I did not send or appoint them. They do not benefit these people in the least," declares the LORD. (Jeremiah 23:32)

In The Morning

_____

_____

_____

_____

_____

_____

_____

SEPTEMBER 24TH

"GETTING DISCOVERED"

You're trying to get into the door. You want the "right" person to help you. Yet - Nothing. Sound familiar?

I get it! You have big goals and big dreams. So why not think that those of influential power and status can help you get there. But what happens when they can't or won't help you?

Remember, just because "they're" not discussing you doesn't mean you won't be discovered!

"I will make you into a great nation, and I will bless you; I will make your name great, and you will be a blessing." (Genesis 12:2)

In The Morning

_____
_____
_____
_____
_____
_____
_____
_____
_____
_____
_____
_____
_____
_____
_____

SEPTEMBER 25TH

"WINNING OR FINISHING"

You want it. And you want it bad. So bad that you'll do anything to get it. Sound familiar?

The truth is there's nothing wrong with winning. But when it looks like you're not going to win, do you still finish the race?

Remember, some folks focus on winning, but few are focused on FINISHING!!!

"I have fought the good fight, I have finished the race, I have kept the faith." (2 Timothy 4:7)

In The Morning

_____
_____
_____
_____
_____
_____
_____
_____
_____
_____
_____
_____
_____
_____
_____

SEPTEMBER 26TH

"WHEN IT RAINS IT POURS"

How many of you are familiar with the saying: When it rains, it pours?

It means that something terrible just happened. And right behind it, something else devastating occurs too.

The truth is rain isn't a bad thing. See, when raindrops fall on the ground where seeds are –it will produce a harvest.

What am I saying? It will always rain right before you REIGN!!!!!!!

"Then I will give you your rains in their season, and the land shall yield its increase, and the trees of the field shall yield their fruit." (Leviticus 26:4)

"You gave abundant showers, O God; you refreshed your weary inheritance." (Psalm 68:9)

In The Morning

SEPTEMBER 27TH

"TEACH THEM YOUR ABSENCE"

Are you always there when someone needs you?

See, it feels good to be needed and wanted. But what happens when you need them, and they are nowhere to be found?

Remember, sometimes you have to teach folks your value by making them learn your absence!

"And as you wish that others would do to you, do so to them." (Luke 6:31)

In The Morning

SEPTEMBER 28TH

"LET ME EXPLAIN"

"I don't think the surgery will be that bad."

"You need to go ahead and get a divorce."

"Natural childbirth will be easier."

See, that's how folks talk when telling you about an experience that they don't know anything about.

Remember, pain explained is NOT the same as pain experienced!

"Therefore, let those who suffer according to God's will entrust their souls to a faithful Creator while doing good." (1 Peter 4:19)

IN THE MORNING

SEPTEMBER 29TH

"YOUR OWN WORST ENEMY"

Are you hard on yourself, and no matter how much others tell you that you can – You tell yourself: "YOU CAN'T!"?

The truth is we can be our own worst enemy. Always putting ourselves down and saying what we can't do. But once we overcome ourselves, then no one can stop us!

Remember, if you don't believe in YOU, how can you expect someone else to?

"For I can do everything through Christ, who gives me strength." (Philippians 4:13)

In The Morning

SEPTEMBER 30TH

"THE TITANIC SUNK"

Some folks think because it's bigger, it's better. But that's not always the case.

See, it's about perception. And perception is not reality, but perception can become a person's reality.

What am I saying: Just because it's bigger doesn't mean it will be better.

Remember, the Titanic was big, beautiful, and shiny; but it also sunk.

"Do not look on his appearance or on the height of his stature, because I have rejected him. For the LORD sees not as man sees; man looks on the outward appearance, but the LORD looks on the heart." (1 Samuel 16:7)

In The Morning

_____

_____

_____

_____

_____

_____

_____

_____

OCTOBER 1ST

"THIS PAIN I HAVE"

Pain is an unpleasant and distressing feeling. Some feel it physically, while others feel it mentally. So which describes you?

See, it doesn't matter which pain you have. Whether big or small – it shouldn't define you.

Remember, your pain is never your final destination. It's just the transportation to where you're going.

"For I consider that the sufferings of this present time are not worth comparing with the glory that is to be revealed to us." (Romans 8:18)

In The Morning

OCTOBER 2ND

"COMPETE WITH ONLY YOU"

Have you ever found yourself trying to beat someone because they were ahead of you?

See, folks often compete with others, while the other party has no clue at all about the competition.

The truth is competition is a sign of insecurity. And if you pursue your own destiny, you won't even have anyone to compete against!

"Pay careful attention to your own work, for then you will get the satisfaction of a job well done, and you won't need to compare yourself to anyone else." (Galatians 6:4)

In The Morning

_____
_____
_____
_____
_____
_____
_____
_____
_____
_____
_____
_____

OCTOBER 3RD

"I'M DISTRACTED"

Being distracted means that you're unable to concentrate because your mind is preoccupied. Now the question you must ask yourself is: What is distracting me?

See, you might not think you're distracted. But if you're not focused and doing what you know, you should be doing. Then you're distracted.

Remember, distraction is a doorway to destruction!!!!

"So let's keep focused on that goal, those of us who want everything God has for us. If any of you have something else in mind, something less than total commitment, God will clear your blurred vision – you'll see it yet!" (Philippians 3:15)

In The Morning

OCTOBER 4TH

"GIVING YOURSELF AWAY"

You want to be there for them, and you're always there when they call. But at what cost?

I get it! You're the "go-to person." But who's there for you?

See, you have to STOP giving the best part of yourself away to folks that wouldn't give you a dime!

Remember, some people in your life don't deserve your best. And you can't make them whole at the expense of you being broken!

"The one stealing, let him steal no longer, but rather let him toil, working with the own hands what is good, so that he may have something to impart to the one having need." (Ephesians 4:28)

IN THE MORNING

_____

_____

_____

_____

_____

_____

_____

_____

_____

_____

_____

_____

OCTOBER 5TH

"HOLDING YOUR HEALING HOSTAGE"

They hurt you and did you wrong. And all you want is an apology. How many can relate?

I get it! You deserve it and are rightfully owed one. But just because you want an apology doesn't mean they will give it to you.

Remember, don't hold your healing hostage by waiting on them to apologize!

"Therefore, confess your sins to one another and pray for one another, that you may be healed. The prayer of a righteous person has great power as it is working." (James 5:16)

In The Morning

OCTOBER 6TH

"THEY PREY...SO YOU PRAY"

Preying is to hunt or take advantage of, ultimately causing trouble and distress. And just because you don't see it, doesn't mean they're not preying on YOU.

See everyone that smiles in your face isn't for you. You have to learn to use discernment and stand on guard. (Ephesians 6:14)

Remember, let them keep preying on you. But you make sure that you stay in PRAYER!!!!!

"Be sober-minded; be watchful. Your adversary, the devil, prowls around like a roaring lion, seeking someone to devour." (1 Peter 5:8)

In The Morning

_____
_____
_____
_____
_____
_____
_____
_____
_____
_____
_____
_____

OCTOBER 7TH

"BLAMING THE SEED"

You planted and sowed it. But now you're mad at what sprouted up. Sound familiar?

The truth is you reap what you sow. And if you don't like what you're reaping, you have to be careful about planting.

Remember, you can't plant wrong and then get mad at the seed planted!

"Do not be deceived: God is not mocked, for whatever one sows, that will he also reap." (Galatians 6:7)

In The Morning

OCTOBER 8TH

"STRUGGLING BUT NOT QUITTING"

You've struggled and been enduring. Yet you're still standing, despite how it looks. Now, how many of YOU have that as your testimony?

The truth is everyone is going to have those days where it's hard to press on. But the difference lies in whether you decide to quit or endure.

Remember, let them see you struggle but NEVER let them see you QUIT!!!!!!

"And let us not grow weary of doing good, for in due season we will reap, if we do not give up." (Galatians 6:9)

In The Morning

OCTOBER 9TH

"CONFRONT IT"

When you're in a confrontation with someone, you're confronting and dealing directly with an issue. The question is: What are you NOT facing in your life?

See, it's one thing to know you have an issue and do something about it. And it's another to know it's there, but never address it.

Remember, you will never heal your wounds if you don't confront them!

"Therefore, confess your sins to one another and pray for one another, that you may be healed. The prayer of a righteous person has great power as it is working." (James 5:16)

In The Morning

_____
_____
_____
_____
_____
_____
_____
_____
_____
_____
_____
_____
_____

OCTOBER 10TH

"BAND-AIDS OR STITCHES"

Have you ever cut yourself and decided to put a Band-Aid on it because it wasn't that bad? But a couple of days later, the wound has gotten worse and infected. Making you realize you need more than a Band-Aid to fix it. Sound familiar?

See, that's how life can be. You have a wound that needs to be taken care of, but you want to put a "Band-Aid" on it and go about your business, leaving the wound infected and unhealed.

Remember, all wounds don't need Band-Aids, some need stitches!!!!!

"Then they cried out to the LORD in their trouble; He saved them out of their distresses. He sent His word and healed them and delivered them from their destructions." (Psalm 107:19-20)

In The Morning

OCTOBER 11TH

"YOU'RE ACTING FUNNY"

You're acting funny is usually a phrase that folks say to you when you don't want to partake in the things you used to do with them.

See, it's okay to act funny. Now I'm not saying be snobbish and stuck up where you think you're better than other people. But know when to say – this isn't me anymore.

Remember, sometimes growing is mistaken as acting funny. And that's okay. Because you should never let ANYONE stunt your growth!!!

"When I was a child, I spoke and thought and reasoned as a child. But when I grew up, I put away childish things." (1 Corinthians 13:11)

In The Morning

_____
_____
_____
_____
_____
_____
_____
_____
_____
_____

OCTOBER 12TH

"TEST IN SESSION: NO TALKING"

You're praying to God, asking Him to rescue you. But yet – NOTHING! How many can relate?

I get it! You want answers RIGHT NOW. And because the answers aren't in the way you expect them, you feel forgotten about, WRONG.

The truth is God hears and sees all. He's not mute to your situation. He will come on time – but you must remain still. (Hebrews 4:13) (2 Chronicles 20:17)

Remember, the teacher never talks during a test!

"Beloved, do not be surprised at the fiery trial when it comes upon you to test you, as though something strange were happening to you. But rejoice insofar as you share Christ's sufferings, that you may also rejoice and be glad when his glory is revealed." (1 Peter 4:12-13)

In The Morning

_____
_____
_____
_____
_____
_____
_____
_____

OCTOBER 13TH

"WALKING OUT OF THE ROOM"

We've all heard the saying, "When one door closes, another one opens." But often, we think the first door that opens is the "ONE." But that's not always the case.

See, you have to learn to test every spirit and use your discernment. Everything isn't always God. (1 John 4:1)

Remember, all doors don't open for you to walk into a room. Some are meant for you to walk OUT of the room!

"And it is my prayer that your love may abound more and more, with knowledge and all discernment," (Philippians 1:9)

In The Morning

OCTOBER 14TH

"WORTHLESS"

They don't value nor appreciate you. And it makes you feel as if you're worthless. Sound familiar?

See, it's a frustrating thing, trying to make others see your worth. And you shouldn't have to keep trying to convince them what they're blind to.

Remember, STOP asking the question, "Why can't they see my worth?" The more significant question is: "Do YOU?"

"Are not five sparrows sold for two pennies? And not one of them is forgotten before God. Why, even the hairs of your head are all numbered. Fear not; you are of more value than many sparrows." (Luke 12:6-7)

In The Morning

_____
_____
_____
_____
_____
_____
_____
_____
_____
_____
_____
_____
_____

OCTOBER 15TH

"IT'S MAKING ME SICK!"

Have you ever done "clean eating"? But then decide to take a cheat day. So you eat unhealthy to where it makes you sick.

See, that's how life can be. You've removed the things that were making you ill. But just like that – you go back to it. And in the end, it causes you to get sick.

Remember, once you start to get healthy, the old way of life you used to feed your stomach might make you sick.

"As a dog returns to its vomit, so fools repeat their folly." (Proverbs 26:11)

In The Morning

OCTOBER 16TH

"DRINKING POISON"

Thirsty is the need of needing a drink of something. But the question is: "What are you thirsty for?"

I get it! It's something that you "think" you want desperately. But at what cost?

Remember, don't be so thirsty that you go back to drinking poison.

"Be sober-minded; be watchful. Your adversary, the devil prowls around like a roaring lion, seeking someone to devour." (1 Peter 5:8)

In The Morning

OCTOBER 17TH

"CLOSED EYES DON'T ERASE YOU"

Have you ever been rejected, left, or thrown away? It's a feeling that no one wants to experience. Unfortunately, we all will deal with some form of rejection in this life.

See, rejection isn't a bad thing. Folk's rejection means God's protection! (Isaiah 41:10) (Proverbs 2:11)

Remember, their closed eyes don't erase YOU!!!!

"As you come to him, the living Stone—rejected by humans but chosen by God and precious to him—" (1 Peter 2:4)

In The Morning

OCTOBER 18TH

"MISQUOTED"

When folks misquote you, they try to report or repeat something that you've said in a way that's not accurate.

So, how many of you have been misquoted?

See, it's a common reaction to want to have a comeback and make a statement about some things. But everything doesn't need to be commented on.

Remember, your silence is the ONLY statement that can't be quoted. If you don't say it, no one can misquote it!

HOLD YOUR PEACE!!!!!!!!

"The Lord will fight for you, and you have only to be silent." (Exodus 14:14)

In The Morning

OCTOBER 19TH

"YOU DON'T LIKE ME, AND I DON'T LIKE YOU"

How many of you care if someone doesn't like you, or are you the one that does the tit for tat with them?

See, some folks want to show that they can be just as lowdown and messy as others. But what's the cost to you when you do stoop that low?

Remember, the moment you hate and do tit for tat with someone back, you become just like them!!!

It's time to be BIGGER & BETTER!!!

"Don't repay evil for evil. Don't retaliate with insults when people insult you. Instead, pay them back with a blessing. That is what God has called you to do, and He will grant you His blessing." (1 Peter 3:9)

IN THE MORNING

OCTOBER 20TH

"REPRESENTING HIM THE WORST"

"I love God."

"Do you love God?"

That's how folks talk and act when they're self-righteous. Meaning they feel like they're the only ones that love and know God only.

See, it's one thing to love and know God, but in secret, purposely misrepresent Him.

Remember, there are times that those who say and claim they know God the BEST will represent Him the WORST!

Don't be them!!!

"They will act religious, but they will reject the power that could make them godly. Stay away from people like that!" (2 Timothy 3:5)

In The Morning

_____
_____
_____
_____
_____
_____
_____
_____
_____

OCTOBER 21ST

"ONE DOOR"

It closed. Slammed and got locked in your face. Sound familiar? See, some folks think because ONE door wasn't for them. That ALL entries are going to be closed to them now. WRONG!!!

Remember, it's the enemy that can trick your mind into convincing you that ONE closed door represents ALL doors. Keep walking! (Ephesians 6:11)

"I know your deeds. See, I have placed before you an open door that no one can shut. I know that you have little strength, yet you have kept my word and have not denied my name." (Revelation 3:8)

In The Morning

OCTOBER 22ND

"BUTTERFLIES WERE ONCE CATERPILLARS"

In life, there are seasons, and what comes with seasons is change. See, you have to learn to move on and not stay stuck in what you once were.

The truth is butterflies were once caterpillars. And some folks will clip their wings to get a caterpillar to notice them.

What do I mean?

STOP cutting and devaluing yourself for other folks from the past. The dead need to remain dead!.

"Therefore, if anyone is in Christ, the new creation has come: The old has gone, the new is here!" (2 Corinthians 5:17)

IN THE MORNING

_____
_____
_____
_____
_____
_____
_____
_____
_____
_____
_____
_____

OCTOBER 23ʳᴰ

"ALL YELLOW BRICK ROADS AREN'T THE PATH HOME"

The Wizard of Oz movie is a classic. And in the film, Dorothy was told to follow the yellow brick road to find her way home.

The question is: How many of you are heading somewhere and trying multiple solutions to get there?

See, just like Dorothy, folks often try multiple paths and people to help them get somewhere. But still – they remain stuck.

Remember, the SOURCE that you're looking for is right under your nose! (1 Corinthians 8:6-8) (AMPC)

"Trust in the Lord with all your heart, and do not lean on your own understanding. In all your ways acknowledge Him, and He will make straight your paths." (Proverbs 3:5-6)

In The Morning

_____
_____
_____
_____
_____
_____
_____
_____
_____

OCTOBER 24TH

"DON'T GET MAD...JUST BE AWARE"

You thought that you knew them. However, they flipped the switch on you. Sound familiar?

The truth is folks are who they are. You can't change them. So there is no need to get upset and frustrated because they showed you the real them.

Remember, when people reveal themselves, don't get mad. Just be aware.

"Beware of false prophets who come disguised as harmless sheep, but are really vicious wolves." (Matthew 7:15)

In The Morning

OCTOBER 25TH

"IT'S ALL I KNOW"

Should I stay, or should I go? That's a question that many find themselves asking when trying to move on.

But the reality of life is, there will come a time that you have to let go. And yes, it might be all you know, but once you release it, God takes it.

Remember, you don't have to stay stuck. God's not calling you backward but forward. (Isaiah 43:18-19)

"Look straight ahead and fix your eyes on what lies before you." (Proverbs 4:25)

In The Morning

_____
_____
_____
_____
_____
_____
_____
_____
_____
_____
_____
_____

OCTOBER 26TH

"STOP AUDITIONING"

When you audition, it's generally for a role in something. Your demonstration of skills and suitability becomes on display for others to judge you to see if you're qualified. The question is: Who are you auditioning for?

See, I'm sure you think that you're not a singer, dancer, musician, or even an actor. So this doesn't apply to you. But it does if you keep trying to audition yourself to be placed in someone's life.

Remember, you have to STOP auditioning for folks who cannot see, appreciate and comprehend what you carry. You're worthy!

"The *one* hearing you hears Me; and the *one* rejecting you rejects Me; and the *one* rejecting Me rejects the *One* having sent Me." (Luke 10:16)

In The Morning

OCTOBER 27TH

"DISCERNMENT"

Discernment is the ability to judge well. And from the Christian context, it's the perception in the absence of judgment to obtain spiritual guidance and understanding.

The question is: Are you using discernment in your life?

See, you have to be able to judge well. If not, anyone can come into your life and disrupt, cause chaos and confusion.

Remember, without you using discernment, you can make a mistake for a "knight" in shining armor with a tin man.

Sound judgment, with discernment, is the best of seers. (Euripides)

"Beloved, do not believe every spirit, but test the spirits to see whether they are from God, for many false prophets have gone out into the world." (1 John 4:1)

In The Morning

OCTOBER 28TH

"CHANGING YOUR SURROUNDINGS"

Have you ever been around some people that you can't stand to be around? But somehow, you stick around them anyways.

See, there comes a time that you have to evaluate your circle. And it's one thing to keep talking about the fools you're around, and it's another not to assess yourself too.

Remember, you can't change the folks around you, but you can change the folks you CHOOSE to be around!!

"Walk with the wise and become wise; associate with fools and get in trouble." (Proverbs 13:20)

In The Morning

OCTOBER 29TH

"ENERGY SUCKERS"

A connection is a relationship in which a person is linked or associated with something else.

Attachment is an extra part of the extension attached to something to perform a particular function.

The question is: Which do you think you're utilizing in your life?

See, to some, they might think connection and attachment are the same things. But it's not.

Remember, you must understand the difference between the two. One will give you power, and the other sucks the life right out of YOU!!!!

"They will act religious, but they will reject the power that could make them godly. Stay away from people like that!" (2 Timothy 3:5)

In The Morning

_____
_____
_____
_____
_____
_____
_____
_____
_____

OCTOBER 30TH

"DIAPERS NEED TO BE CHANGED"

You want them to change, but they remain the same, no matter how much you push them. Sound familiar?

See, you can drive yourself crazy trying to make someone be something they're not ready to be.

But at the end of the day, they have to WANT TO make the change, not YOU.

Remember, you change diapers, NOT people!

"Whoever remains stiff-necked after many rebukes will suddenly be destroyed—without remedy." (Proverbs 29:1)

In The Morning

OCTOBER 31ST

"NEW PEOPLE, SAME ISSUES"

You left, and in some cases, escaped what meant you no good. So how is it that you ended up back in the same cycle?

I get it! It's familiar and what you know. But just because it's what you know doesn't mean it's right for you.

Remember, it's time to break the cycle!!!! You can't keep picking new folks with the same issues. Familiar doesn't mean good when the past was TOXIC!!!!!

"They hit me," you will say, "but I'm not hurt! They beat me, but I don't feel it! When will I wake up so I can find another drink?" Do not envy the wicked, do not desire their company;" (Proverbs 23:35) (Proverbs 24:1)

In The Morning

_____
_____
_____
_____
_____
_____
_____
_____
_____
_____
_____
_____

NOVEMBER 1ST

"CUTTING THE UMBILICAL CORD"

Umbilical cords are a flexible cordlike structure containing blood vessels attaching human or other mammalian fetuses to the placenta during gestation. When a mother gives birth to a newborn baby and the umbilical cord is connected, you see this. The question is: Have you cut your umbilical cord yet?

See, many folks think because they're not pregnant, this doesn't apply to them. But it does if you're still attached and holding on to unforgiveness from the past.

Remember, unforgiveness is just like an umbilical cord. It will keep you attached to the womb of what happened in the past.

It's time to cut the "cord" so you can heal and grow!

"Let all bitterness and wrath and anger and clamor and slander be put away from you, along with all malice. Be kind to one another, tenderhearted, forgiving one another, as God in Christ forgave you." (Ephesians 4:31-32)

In The Morning

_____
_____
_____
_____
_____
_____
_____
_____

NOVEMBER 2ND

"YOU HAVE TO GET CUT"

"Glory"

"Accolades"

"Notoriety"

Now, is that what you're seeking? See, many want the shine and the greatness. But they don't want to go through the hell it took to get it.

Remember, if you want to be a diamond, prepare to get cut.

"Do you see what I've done? I've refined you, but not without fire. I've tested you like silver in the furnace of affliction." (Isaiah 48:10)

IN THE MORNING

NOVEMBER 3ʳᴰ

"GUARD YOUR GARDEN"

Gardens are small pieces of ground used to grow vegetables, fruits, herbs, or flowers. The question is: Have you ever thought about yourself being a garden?

See, your "garden" is an area that you grow and blossom in, but if you don't take care of it, you can't expect it to bloom.

Remember, it's time to guard your garden. If not – You might get kicked out because of who or what you let in!

"You are a garden spring, a well of fresh water, streams flowing from Lebanon." (Song of Solomon 4:15)

In The Morning

NOVEMBER 4TH

"THE INNER – YOU"

How many times have you been quick to say, "That's the enemy causing this?"

I get it! The enemy's job is to steal, kill and destroy. (John 10:10) But what about the things you do to yourself?

The truth is everything isn't the enemy. There comes a time that YOU have to take responsibility for your actions that caused your situation.

Remember, all attacks aren't the result of the enemy, but the result of the INNER-YOU!

"For we must all appear before the judgment seat of Christ, so that each one may receive what is due for what he has done in the body, whether good or evil." (2 Corinthians 5:10)

In The Morning

_____

_____

_____

_____

_____

_____

_____

_____

_____

NOVEMBER 5TH

"PROTECT YOUR EARS"

As soon as they open their mouth and start talking, it's negative, gloomy, and pessimistic. Sound familiar?

See, that's just how some folks are. They're negative! This is why you must protect your ears.

Remember, sometimes you have to say, "You might not be done talking, but I'm done listening."

"Tune your ears to wisdom and concentrate on understanding." (Proverbs 2:2)

In The Morning

NOVEMBER 6TH

"THEY'RE MAD AT YOU FOR BEING WHOLE"

Have you ever tried to share your good news with a family member or a friend? But they have an attitude as if they could care less about your joy.

I get it! You're close to them, and you expect them to be happy for you. But the reason they don't share in your happiness has nothing to do with you, but them!

Remember, some people are so broken that they become angry with you for being WHOLE!

"Do not make friends with a hot-tempered person, do not associate with one easily angered, or you may learn their ways and get yourself ensnared." (Proverbs 22:24-25)

In The Morning

_____
_____
_____
_____
_____
_____
_____
_____
_____
_____
_____
_____

NOVEMBER 7ᵀᴴ

"EATING FROM EVERY PLATE"

Have you ever been hungry and received multiple invitations to come and eat? And when you finally choose a place to dine, it's not what you think.

See, all invites aren't for you to attend. That's why it's imperative to use discernment. (Hebrews 5:14 ESV)

Remember, never be so hungry that you eat from every plate that's prepared for you. If so – you'll end up poisoned!

"Do not crave that ruler's delicacies, for that food is deceptive." (Proverbs 23:3 NET)

In The Morning

NOVEMBER 8TH

"WAIT-TRAINING"

Weight training is physical training that involves lifting weights over some time to get the results that you want. However, the results don't come overnight.

The question is, "How much "Wait-Training" are you going to put in with your trials? (James 5:7-8 ESV)

Remember, the day you plant the seed is not the day you eat the fruit. Be patient and stay the course. (Fabienne Fredrickson)

"But they who wait for the Lord shall renew their strength; they shall mount up with wings like eagles; they shall run and not be weary; they shall walk and not faint." (Isaiah 40:31 ESV)

In The Morning

_____
_____
_____
_____
_____
_____
_____
_____
_____
_____
_____
_____
_____

NOVEMBER 9TH

"DIRTY HANDS"

"Did you see what she did?" "Look at them – and they have no right to be doing that."

See, that's how folks talk that's always pointing the finger at others. But that's not YOU, is it?

I get it. They're in the wrong, and you want others to know. But who has appointed you judge and jury?

Remember, it's always the ones with dirty hands that are quick to point their finger at others!

"Do not judge, or you too will be judged." (Matthew 7:1 NIV)

In The Morning

NOVEMBER 10TH

"BETTER IS COMING"

Have you ever been upset because "it" didn't work out? Then have an attitude of "woe is me"?

I get it; no one wants to face disappointment, but all disappointments aren't bad.

Remember, God will NEVER take away His best! Better IS coming!!!!

"And we know that God causes everything to work together for the good of those who love God and are called according to His purpose for them." (Romans 8:28 NLT)

In The Morning

NOVEMBER 11TH

"YOUR WORDS CAN CHANGE YOU"

It's one thing when folks talk down to you and about you. But what happens when you're the one that's always putting yourself down?

I get it! You're hard on yourself. However, what you say about yourself is what you're declaring.

Remember, your words can change you. So don't ruin your mind and mood with the words you speak!

"Death and life are in the power of the tongue, and those who love it will eat its fruits." (Proverbs 18:21)

In The Morning

_____
_____
_____
_____
_____
_____
_____
_____
_____
_____
_____
_____
_____
_____
_____

NOVEMBER 12ᵀᴴ

"RESURRECTING THE DEAD"

You've prayed about it and asked God to renew and restore it. Yet nothing has taken place. Sound familiar?

The truth is God hears and sees all. Your prayers are being answered. They might just come differently than how you expected them. (Psalm 66:17-20)

Remember, sometimes you have to accept that God isn't going to revive what He killed in your life. It's DEAD! Please STOP trying to resurrect it!

"I will not pasture you. What is to die, let it die, and what is to be annihilated, let it be annihilated." (Zechariah 11:9)

In The Morning

_____

_____

_____

_____

_____

_____

_____

_____

_____

_____

NOVEMBER 13TH

"STOP MONITORING IT"

You say you're going to give it over to the Lord. But you keep picking it back up. Now surely that isn't YOU, is it?

I get it! You want to handle it and try to fix it yourself. But if you're going to do it. Why do you need God at all?

Remember, STOP monitoring what you've already turned over to God! If you say you trust Him, then TRUST HIM ONLY!!!!!

"And this is the confidence that we have before Him: If we ask anything according to His will, He hears us." (1 John 5:14)

In The Morning

NOVEMBER 14TH

"THE GOODBYE"

Have you ever had to tell someone goodbye? And you didn't want to. But keeping them was hurting you more.

See, in life, hard decisions have to be made. And even though you might not want to do it, it's necessary.

Remember, when you say goodbye, it clears room and space for what is to come.

"There is a time for everything, and a season for every activity under the heavens: a time to be born and a time to die, a time to plant and a time to uproot," (Ecclesiastes 3:1-2)

In The Morning

NOVEMBER 15TH

"BUT THEY CAN'T SEE IT"

Have you ever been looking outside and saw that it was raining? But then someone looks right out behind you and says that they don't see anything? But you know that it is.

See to you, it's raining. But to them, it might be sprinkling. So they don't consider it is raining.

What am I saying? Just because they don't see it, doesn't mean it's not there!!

"Open my eyes, that I may behold wondrous things out of your law." (Psalm 119:18)

IN THE MORNING

NOVEMBER 16TH

"FULL ATTITUDE BUT HALF THE FACTS"

"She said" "He said" "They said"
Those are all common phrases used when people start to gossip.

The truth is folks are going to talk, no matter what. But the question is, "Are you getting mad when you don't know if the gossip is true?"

Remember, you have to stop catching full attitudes with half the facts!

"Do not spread false reports. Do not help a guilty person by being a malicious witness." (Exodus 23:1)

In The Morning

NOVEMBER 17TH

"RUBBING ME THE WRONG WAY"

When you want your furniture or silverware to shine, you have to polish it. So it's going to require some rubbing to get that smooth and shiny glow.

But have you ever thought about how you get polished daily?

See, some folks might test you. Even work your last nerves and rub you the wrong way. And that's okay! You have to make sure you don't react to it.

Why? Because you're being polished!!!

"You are the light of the world. A city set on a hill cannot be hidden. Nor do people light a lamp and put it under a basket, but on a stand, and it gives light to all in the house." (Matthew 5:14-15)

IN THE MORNING

NOVEMBER 18TH

"GENERATIONAL CURSES"

Because your mother, father, or grandmother did it. You've taken it on too. Sound familiar?

See, bad habits are just that: they're bad habits!!! There's no need to keep blaming what your family did on your OWN choices now.

Remember, some issues that you're quick to call generational curses are your bad habits.

"No temptation has overtaken you that is not common to man. God is faithful, and He will not let you be tempted beyond your ability, but with the temptation, He will also provide the way of escape, that you may be able to endure it." (1 Corinthians 10:13)

IN THE MORNING

NOVEMBER 19TH

"BE AN ELEVATOR"

Have you ever been on an elevator and want to go to the 12th floor? But the person next to you is getting off on the 4th. So before the elevator gets to your destination, it has to stop to let the other person off. Sound familiar?

See, in life, you have to know when it's time to let people go. Why? Because there are just some folks that shouldn't go to the top with you.

"Whoever walks with the wise becomes wise, but the companion of fools will suffer harm." (Proverbs 13:20)

In The Morning

NOVEMBER 20TH

"TRYING TO GO BACK IN THE SHELL"

Broken is being fractured or damaged and no longer in one piece or working order. The question is: What broke you, and are you trying to go back to it?

See, when you're broken, it's a hurt and awful feeling. But you can cause more hurt by going back to what broke you.

Remember, you can never put a broken egg back in its shell.

"Like a dog that returns to his vomit is a fool who repeats his folly." (Proverbs 26:11)

"Brothers and sisters, I do not consider myself yet to have taken hold of it. But one thing I do: Forgetting what is behind and straining toward what is ahead," (Philippians 3:13)

In The Morning

_____
_____
_____
_____
_____
_____
_____
_____
_____
_____
_____
_____

NOVEMBER 21ST

"GOD DOESN'T LOSE"

How many are you quick to say that you're giving your battles to God but pick it back up?

See, when you turn everything over to Him. It means you're putting complete faith in God to work it out.

Remember, God hasn't lost a battle yet, so let it go and let Him fight for you.

"You will not have to fight this battle. Take up your positions; stand firm and see the deliverance the LORD will give you, Judah and Jerusalem. Do not be afraid; do not be discouraged. Go out to face them tomorrow, and the LORD will be with you.'" (2 Chronicles 20:17)

IN THE MORNING

_____

_____

_____

_____

_____

_____

_____

_____

_____

_____

_____

_____

NOVEMBER 22ND

"EYES LIKE A LION"

A lion's eyesight is by far their most important sense. And at night, it's exceptionally superior. The question is: How are your eyes when it gets dark?

See, I'm sure you think that when it's dark, it's time to close your eyes. Especially at nighttime. But what are you doing when "life" gets dark for you.

Remember, sometimes you have to be like a lion and not lose sight when dark times come.

"Even the darkness is not dark to you; the night is bright as the day, for darkness is as light with you." (Psalm 139:12)

In The Morning

_____
_____
_____
_____
_____
_____
_____
_____
_____
_____
_____
_____

NOVEMBER 23RD

"LEFTOVERS"

Leftovers are something, especially food, that remains after the rest has been used or consumed. The question is: Are you being treated like a leftover?

See, you probably think that you're not food, so you know this doesn't apply to you. But it does if you keep allowing folks to use you.

Remember, you have to STOP giving people in your life do-overs if all they're doing is treating you like a leftover!

"Remove the false way from me, And graciously grant me Your law." (Psalm 119:29)

In The Morning

NOVEMBER 24TH

"DON'T PUT YOUR GIFT IN THE WRONG HANDS"

You're gifted and talented. Yet, you feel as if your gift is stressing you out. Sound familiar?

See, every good and perfect gift is from above. So if your gift(s) is stressing you, maybe it's because of you. (James 1:17)

Remember, sometimes your gifts will feel like a curse if they're placed in the wrong hands.

Protect your gifts!!!!!!!

"Do not be negligent of the gift in you." (1 Timothy 4:14)

In The Morning

NOVEMBER 25TH

"A GLOSSY PIT"

Decorating is when you want to make "something" look more attractive by adding some extra items or images to it. The question is: Are you being fooled by the decorations?

See, it doesn't matter if it's a place, person, or thing. When it's all decorated and shiny, it can appear to be the "perfect" thing. But is it really?

Remember, STOP letting the decorations fool you. A pit is still a pit, even if it's glossy!

"In the same way, on the outside you appear to people as righteous, but on the inside you are full of hypocrisy and wickedness." (Matthew 23:28)

In The Morning

_____
_____
_____
_____
_____
_____
_____
_____
_____
_____
_____
_____
_____

NOVEMBER 26TH

"COMMITTED TO YOUR PAST OR FUTURE?"

The past is gone by in time and no longer exists. The future is time regarded as still to come.

So which are you seeking?

YES! The past has memories that are to be cherished and sometimes hard to forget. But you have to let go of what was and embrace what's to come at some point.

Remember, you can't be committed to both your past and the future at the same time. Either you choose one, or it will select YOU!!!

"Forget the former things; do not dwell on the past. See, I am doing a new thing! Now it springs up; do you not perceive it? I am making a way in the wilderness and streams in the wasteland." (Isaiah 43:18-19)

In The Morning

_____

_____

_____

_____

_____

_____

_____

_____

NOVEMBER 27TH

"DID YOU LET IT GO OR BURY IT?"

Letting go is to stop holding on to something or someone. To bury is to cover- hide down completely. The question is: Which are you doing?

See, it's easy to say you've let go. But have you really, if all you're doing is burying the pain?

Remember, often, what you think you're letting go of, is actually being buried, and what's buried will grow!!!

"Sow for yourselves righteousness; reap steadfast love; break up your fallow ground, for it is the time to seek the LORD, that He may come and rain righteousness upon you." (Hosea 10:12)

IN THE MORNING

NOVEMBER 28TH

"LET IT RAIN"

Rain is nothing but water droplets from the clouds. And clouds can cause gloom, suspicion, trouble, or worry. The question is: Are you okay when the rain comes?

See, rain isn't a bad thing. Yes, you're going to become wet if you don't have coverage. But the rain causes your seed to grow.

What do I mean? The same folks that tried to destroy you and brought the storms in your life. They had no clue you would blossom when the rain came.

"Shower, O heavens, from above, and let the clouds rain down righteousness; let the earth open, that salvation and righteousness may bear fruit; let the earth cause them both to sprout; I, the LORD, have created it." (Isaiah 45:8)

IN THE MORNING

___
___
___
___
___
___
___
___
___
___
___
___

NOVEMBER 29TH

"WHAT IS YOUR ATTITUDE SAYING?"

Energy is your mental activity. And attitude is your way of thinking or behavior. The question is: How are you coming off?

See, sometimes folks think because they don't say anything, it's okay. But they forget their attitude is speaking.

Remember, your energy will always introduce you before you open your mouth.

"Let the Spirit renew your thoughts and attitudes." (Ephesians 4:23)

IN THE MORNING

NOVEMBER 30TH

"USE YOUR KEYS WISELY"

Keys are something that most people have. Whether it's to their homes, cars, or lockers, they're used to open and lock doors.

The question is: Are you using them wisely?

Remember, make sure you use your keys daily to open new possibilities, lock out old problems, and grant access to what God has placed in you!!!

"Ask, and it will be given to you; seek, and you will find; knock, and it will be opened to you. For everyone who asks receives, and the one who seeks finds, and to the one who knocks it will be opened." (Matthew 7:7-8)

In The Morning

_____
_____
_____
_____
_____
_____
_____
_____
_____
_____
_____

DECEMBER 1ST

"YOUR "YES" DOESN'T NEED COUNSEL"

God gave you a "YES," and you've accepted it. But folks are trying to tell you otherwise. Sound familiar?

See, folks always have something to say. So let them talk. Because what they say will never trump over God's Word.

Remember, God has given you favor for a "YES." No one can CANCEL or COUNSEL you out of His "YES"!

"God is not a man, that He should lie, or a son of man, that He should change His mind. Does He speak and not act? Does He promise and not fulfill?" (Numbers 23:19)

IN THE MORNING

_____
_____
_____
_____
_____
_____
_____
_____
_____
_____
_____
_____

DECEMBER 2ND

"THE LETDOWN"

Have you ever been let down, hurt or disappointed? And because of the hurt, you didn't know what to do next. Sound familiar?

See, in life, disappointments are going to come. But it's how you deal with them that matters.

Remember, never allow your "letdown" to shut you down!!!!

"We are pressed on every side by troubles, but we are not crushed. We are perplexed, but not driven to despair. We are hunted down, but never abandoned by God. We get knocked down, but we are not destroyed." (2 Corinthians 4:8-9)

In The Morning

_____

_____

_____

_____

_____

_____

_____

_____

_____

_____

_____

_____

DECEMBER 3ᴿᴰ

"SABOTAGING THE SHIP"

When folks want to destroy, damage, or obstruct something deliberately, they sabotage it! The question is: What are you sabotaging in your own life?

See, you may not be aware that you're doing something on purpose. But if you're continually pushing away who or what was sent to help you – that's sabotage!

Remember, STOP sabotaging the ship that was sent to rescue YOU! (Luke 5:3-10)

"Pride goes before destruction, and a haughty spirit before a fall." (Proverbs 16:18)

In The Morning

_____
_____
_____
_____
_____
_____
_____
_____
_____
_____
_____

DECEMBER 4TH

"A PROTECTED HEART"

You have given your heart to this one and that one. Yet, it's been broken repeatedly. Sound familiar?

See, no one wants a broken heart. And a person has every right to protect who they give their heart to.

So the best way to protect your heart – is to give it to God and let Him QUALIFY who deserves the space in it!

"Give me your heart, my son, And let your eyes delight in my ways." (Proverbs 23:26)

In The Morning

___
___
___
___
___
___
___
___
___
___
___
___
___
___
___
___
___

DECEMBER 5TH

"THE STALKER"

God removed it. Yet, you still can't let it go. Sound familiar? I get it. You wanted it and didn't want it to go or end. But it did. So now what?

Now you leave it alone!

Remember, when God blocks it, you don't need to stalk it!!!

"The LORD keeps you from all harm and watches over your life." (Psalm 121:7)

In The Morning

DECEMBER 6ᵀᴴ

"BUT YOU GOT WHAT YOU WANTED"

You wanted it badly. But when you finally got it. It wasn't what you expected. Sound familiar?

See, everything isn't as it seems. And what you "THOUGHT" was going to be a blessing. Can end up hurting and harming you.

Remember, everything isn't God-sent!

"Stay alert! Watch out for your great enemy, the devil. He prowls around like a roaring lion, looking for someone to devour." (1 Peter 5:8)

In The Morning

DECEMBER 7TH

"ARE YOU GOING TO BE IN FAITH OR YOUR FEELINGS?"

Faith is confidence in what we hope for and assurance about what we do not see. (Hebrews 11:1) Feelings are your emotional state. The question is: Which are you leading with?

See, folks can be cruel and mean – causing your feelings to hurt. But just because they threw the "stone" doesn't mean you have to react to it. (Proverbs 28:26)

Remember, you have to let your faith be more significant than your feelings.

"For God gave us a spirit, not of fear but of power and love and self-control." (2 Timothy 1:7)

In The Morning

_____
_____
_____
_____
_____
_____
_____
_____
_____
_____

DECEMBER 8TH

"THEIR OPINION BUT YOUR ASSIGNMENT"

You had the vision and ran with it. But someone had something to say about it. So you stopped. Sound familiar?

See, folks are always going to have something to say. If you didn't do it, they would claim, "You're lazy." And if you did do it, "You're doing too much."

So do YOU!

Remember, don't let the opinions of others STOP the assignment God has called you for.

"For this reason I remind you to fan into flame the gift of God, which is in you through the laying on of my hands." (2 Timothy 1:6)

IN THE MORNING

DECEMBER 9TH

"OUT OF VIP"

When a person is in the VIP section, they're entitled to many perks—making it the place to be. But then you have the balcony section, which is in the back. And it's the worst spot to be.

The question is: Where are you allowing folks in your life?

See, I'm sure you think you don't have a stage or auditorium. So this doesn't apply to you. But it does if you keep allowing folks to be in your life that shouldn't be.

Remember, there are times that you just need to up and move some people from the VIP section of your life and sit them in a regular balcony seat!!!

"No one can serve two masters; for either he will hate the one and love the other, or he will be devoted to the one and despise the other. You cannot serve God and mammon [money, possessions, fame, status, or whatever is valued more than the Lord]." (Matthew 6:24)(AMP)

In The Morning

_____
_____
_____
_____
_____
_____
_____
_____

DECEMBER 10TH

"THE OBSESSION"

When a person is obsessed, they're preoccupied with the state of being with someone or something. The question is: Are you obsessed?

See, it's a knee-jerk reaction to say no. But if you can't stop watching and lurking into what others are doing – you're obsessed!

Remember, you will never find out the life you should have if you become obsessed with everyone else's.

BE YOU!!!!!!!!

"Do not love the world or the things in the world. If anyone loves the world, the love of the Father is not in him. For all that is in the world—the desires of the flesh and the desires of the eyes and pride in possessions—is not from the Father but is from the world. And the world is passing away along with its desires, but whoever does the will of God abides forever." (1 John 2:15-17)

In The Morning

_____
_____
_____
_____
_____
_____
_____
_____

DECEMBER 11ᵀᴴ

"LET THEM BE MAD"

Have you ever come across someone that didn't like you? And you had no reason at all why they felt the way they did.

See, some folk's attitude and hatred towards you have nothing to do with you. It's all about them.

So don't apologize for the favor over your life. Let them be mad.

"For you bless the righteous, O LORD; you cover him with favor as with a shield." (Psalm 5:12)

In The Morning

DECEMBER 12TH

"FIGHT FOR IT"

Marriage. Job. Family. Relationships. From every which way you turn, you're catching hell. And because of it, you're ready to give up. Sound familiar?

See, there are some things in life that you must walk away from. Then there are things that you have to fight for.

Remember, everything isn't toxic. That's why you must lean on the Lord and listen for discernment. It could be you're under attack!!!! (1 Kings 3:9)

"For we do not wrestle against flesh and blood, but against the rulers, against the authorities, against the cosmic powers over this present darkness, against the spiritual forces of evil in the heavenly places." (Ephesians 6:12)

IN THE MORNING

DECEMBER 13TH

"THE KNOW-IT-ALL"

They came into your life to help you. But because you're a know-it-all, you're not trying to receive anything they say. Sound familiar?

See, it's a dangerous thing for a person to know EVERYTHING and can't be taught. The teacher will rise when the student is ready.

The question is: Are you ready?

Remember, don't let you and your attitude hate on the person that God sent to bless you. Learn to close your mouth before your door gets closed!!!!

"Arrogant know-it-alls stir up discord, but wise men and women listen to each other's counsel." (Proverbs 13:10)

In The Morning

_____
_____
_____
_____
_____
_____
_____
_____
_____
_____

DECEMBER 14TH

"JUST SAY NO!"

They want you to do something, and you say yes.

They call, and you take off running.

They need, and you're there for the want.

Sound familiar?

See, some folks in this world can drain you dry. But that's not on them. It's on YOU for allowing them to.

Remember, there comes a time that you have to stop saying YES to everything and just say NO!!!!!

"You say, "I am allowed to do anything"—but not everything is good for you. And even though "I am allowed to do anything," I must not become a slave to anything." (1 Corinthians 6:12)

In The Morning

DECEMBER 15ᵀᴴ

"THE ANOINTED"

The anointing is what empowers a man or a woman to function in their authority supernaturally.

The question is: Are you anointed?

See, the oil costs. And some folks think because you're anointed, you're exempt from trials and tribulations. WRONG!

Remember, the fact that "they" don't like you, won't make you unanointed.

"Do not touch my anointed ones; do my prophets no harm."" (Psalm 105:15)

In The Morning

_____
_____
_____
_____
_____
_____
_____
_____
_____
_____
_____
_____
_____
_____

DECEMBER 16TH

"TAKE THE MEDICINE PLEASE"

When someone is sick, it's usually medicine that would be the cure to heal them. But what happens when they refuse to take the meds?

The truth is you can't force someone to be healed. They have to want it for themselves.

Remember, you can't keep bringing medicine to folks who love being sick.

"And if anyone will not receive you or listen to your words, shake off the dust from your feet when you leave that house or town." (Matthew 10:14)

In The Morning

DECEMBER 17TH

"CONTROL YOUR OWN THERMOSTAT"

Sometimes, when you're in a room, someone might be cold, and another might be hot. And before you know it, someone will try to go and adjust the thermostat.

See, that's how life can be. You're "HOT" about the situation, and the other person is feeling another kind of way about it. And before you know it – You blow up!!!

Remember, you must learn to control your thermostat only. Otherwise, your temperament will act accordingly to how others adjust the knob!

"He who is slow to anger is better than a warrior, and he who controls his temper is greater than one who captures a city." (Proverbs 16:32)

In The Morning

___
___
___
___
___
___
___
___
___
___
___

DECEMBER 18TH

"LET IT PLAY OUT"

"Worrying."

"Not sleeping."

"Trying to do EVERYTHING to fix it."

Sound Familiar?

I get it! You THINK you don't know what to do. But you do. {Turn it over to the Lord} (Philippians 4:6-7)

Remember, be patient while this plays out. And STOP losing your mind over something that God has already worked OUT!!!!

"But Jesus answered them, "To this very day My Father is at His work, and I too am working." (John 5:17)

IN THE MORNING

_____
_____
_____
_____
_____
_____
_____
_____
_____
_____
_____

DECEMBER 19TH

"DON'T LET THE ACCIDENT BE YOUR CHOICE!"

You fell, and in some cases, the fall wasn't your fault.

How many can relate?

See, you can't control the cards that you're dealt in life. They're your cards. But how you play your hand is what matters.

Remember, the "fall" might have been an accident. But staying down is on YOU!!!!

"Though I have fallen, I will arise." (Micah 7:8)

In The Morning

DECEMBER 20TH

"THE POWER OF STEPPING AWAY"

When a match is struck, friction creates heat, and a flammable compound ignites in the air. So, if a book of matches gets lit, it will result in a fire through a chain reaction.

Now, the question you have to ask is: What will happen if one match removed itself from the book? (it wouldn't get burned)

See, sometimes you have to step away from the FIRE, so it doesn't harm you.

Remember, you might not have caused the fire, but just being in the mix can cause you to get burned!

"Walk away from the company of fools, for you cannot find insight in their words. It takes wisdom for the clever to understand the path they are on, but the fool is deceived by his own foolishness." (Proverbs 14:7-8) The Voice (VOICE)

In The Morning

_____
_____
_____
_____
_____
_____
_____
_____

DECEMBER 21ST

"GROWN UPS"

"I'm grown!"

Now that's what a millennial usually yells at their parents when they're trying to prove a point that they're no longer a child.

But truth be told – Some adults often try to use their age to show that they're older too. But are they really?

See, just because a person is of age doesn't necessarily mean that they're older. (Wiser)

Remember, aging is automatic. But growth is a choice.

"When I was a child, I spoke and thought and reasoned as a child. But when I grew up, I put away childish things." (1 Corinthians 13:11)

IN THE MORNING

DECEMBER 22ND

"BITING YOUR TONGUE"

Have you ever wanted to say something, but you knew you shouldn't?

See, it might feel good to get "it" off your chest. But that doesn't mean that's what you should do. Instead, you need to sit there and be still, smile, and turn it over to the Lord. (Exodus 14:14)

Remember, the discipline is in NOT saying what you WANT to say.

"Watch your tongue and keep your mouth shut, and you will stay out of trouble." (Proverbs 21:23)

In The Morning

DECEMBER 23RD

"EXPECTING YOU FROM OTHER FOLKS"

Let's face it – having your heart broken hurts. But what happens when the person that keeps breaking your heart is none other than yourself? (YOU)

See, it's easy to blame others when they keep hurting and causing you pain. But are you accepting fault when you keep causing the pain?

Remember, sometimes you end up breaking your own heart by expecting folks to be just like YOU! (TRUE & LOYAL)

So, apologize to yourself for expecting YOU from other folks!

"Only take care, and keep your soul diligently, lest you forget the things that your eyes have seen, and lest they depart from your heart all the days of your life. Make them known to your children and your children's children" (Deuteronomy 4:9)

In The Morning

___
___
___
___
___
___
___
___

DECEMBER 24TH

"STINKIN' THINKIN'"

"I don't think I can do it."

"This is going to be too hard for me."

"I will never make it."

See, that's the thought process of what someone says when they're thinking negatively.

The question is, does that fit YOU?

The truth is you're only going to go as far as your attitude permits. So, if you say you can, YOU WILL. If you say you can't, YOU WON'T!

Remember, if you continue with your "stinkin' thinkin'," you will stay stinkin' stuck! And to go to new levels, you must change the way you think!!!!

"I can do all things through Christ who gives me strength." (Philippians 4:13)

In The Morning

_____
_____
_____
_____
_____
_____
_____
_____
_____

DECEMBER 25ᵀᴴ

"THE RUNAWAY"

The past can make some folks laugh, and others might cry. Then you have those that light up like a Christmas Tree. But not everyone loves reminiscing about the good ole days.

I get it! Who wants to rekindle the hurt and pain from the past? But if you continue to run away from it – it will only make the pain drag out further.

Remember, you can run, but no matter how far and fast you do – Eventually, you'll have to address the pain from your past!

"The wicked run away when no one is chasing them, but the godly are as bold as lions." (Proverbs 28:1) (NLT)

In The Morning

_____
_____
_____
_____
_____
_____
_____
_____
_____
_____
_____
_____

DECEMBER 26TH

"CHANGE YOUR FLAT TIRE"

Have you ever had a flat tire? See, when you get a flat tire, you have to change it. If not, you can cause internal structural damage to the tire, leading to the wheel and resulting in poor handling and control of the vehicle—ultimately causing an accident.

So, how many of you have "flat tires" in your life that need to be changed?

I get it. You probably think I don't have a flat tire - But if you have a bad attitude or think negatively, that's a "flat tire." And it needs to be changed immediately!

Remember, negative attitudes are like flat tires; if you don't change it, you won't be going ANYWHERE!!!!!!

"Refrain from anger and abandon wrath; do not fret--it can only bring harm." (Psalm 37:8)

In The Morning

_____
_____
_____
_____
_____
_____
_____
_____
_____

DECEMBER 27TH

"STICKS & STONES"

Some folks are known to throw rocks and hide their hands. But surely that isn't you, is it?

I get it! You want them to hurt. But vengeance is mine says the Lord. (Romans 12:19)

Remember, sticks and stones thrown, can break bones, but your TOXIC words will fracture the mind!

"I tell you, on the day of judgment, people will give account for every careless word they speak, for by your words you will be justified, and by your words you will be condemned." (Matthew 12:36-37)

In The Morning

DECEMBER 28TH

"WHO'S REALLY WITH ME?"

Folks, friends, and even family can be wishy-washy. They can be there one minute and gone the next.

Leaving the million-dollar question: Who's really with me?

The truth is "they" can walk out of your life at any given moment. But there is someone closer than no other. (Proverbs 18:24)

Remember, people can and will leave. BUT GOD will NEVER leave YOU!!!!

"Be strong and courageous. Do not be afraid or terrified because of them, for the Lord your God goes with you; He will never leave you nor forsake you." (Deuteronomy 31:6**)**

In The Morning

_____
_____
_____
_____
_____
_____
_____
_____
_____
_____
_____
_____

DECEMBER 29TH

"OWN YOUR PART"

"It's the enemy!"
"The devil did it!"

Now how many of you are continually throwing blame at the devil?

The truth is there are some things that the enemy is the root of, but have you ever thought about the role you play in it?

Remember, you must own your part. Sometimes it's YOUR decision(s) and NOT the devil!

"Understanding is a wellspring of life unto him that hath it: but the instruction of fools is folly." (Proverbs 16:22)

In The Morning

_____
_____
_____
_____
_____
_____
_____
_____
_____
_____
_____
_____

DECEMBER 30TH

"IT COULD'VE BEEN YOU"

They fell, but you laughed.

Now surely that isn't you, is it?

See, to some folks watching others fall is funny. But what happens when the person that's falling is YOU?

So, instead of laughing, gossiping, and running them down in the ground. Choose to cover them in prayer and NOT exposure.

Remember, it could've been YOU!

"Let no corrupting talk come out of your mouths, but only such as is good for building up, as fits the occasion, that it may give grace to those who hear." (Ephesians 4:29)

In The Morning

_____
_____
_____
_____
_____
_____
_____
_____
_____
_____
_____

DECEMBER 31ST

"WHICH ONE: SURGERY OR PAIN KILLERS?"

They ask you if you want the truth or the lie. You say the truth. But when you get it, you go berserk.

Now surely that isn't you, is it?

Remember, the truth can be like surgery. It might hurt - but it will cure you. A lie is like painkillers. It will give you temporary relief - but the side effects are forever.

"Truthful lips endure forever, but a lying tongue is but for a moment." (Proverbs 12:19)

In The Morning

_____
_____
_____
_____
_____
_____
_____
_____
_____
_____
_____
_____
_____
_____
_____
_____

ABOUT THE AUTHOR

Travasa Holloway is the owner of TNHB Inspirations. She is a Henderson, Kentucky native and resides now in South Carolina. Ms. Holloway is the proud mother of twin sons, Ra'Mon (Ray) & Rod Holloway, and the grandmother of two granddaughters Avaya & Kalani Holloway. She has been in advertising for over 24 years.

Ms. Holloway began writing from a personal healing place, which later became a healing place for others. She reaches thousands of readers through her daily devotionals as TNHB Inspirations, and she continues to be invited to speak to share her inspirational journey with others throughout the country. It's her hope and prayer that In The Morning, others too will find their inner strength.

For speaking engagements and purchases, you may contact the author at:

tnhb@tnhb-inspirations.com

www.tnhb-inspirations.com

www.ingramcontent.com/pod-product-compliance
Lightning Source LLC
Chambersburg PA
CBHW051416290426
44109CB00016B/1322